GW01377088

For Olive

SIR DAVID MARTIN

Thank you for your hospitality and many kindnesses. I know Lee always remembers my 1997 trip to Ireland and to Clare and Spellycrone especially.

Love and thanks

Anasea Kennedy
1997.

SIR DAVID MARTIN
A Man of Courage and Dedication

MAREA STENMARK
FOREWORD BY SIR NINIAN STEPHEN

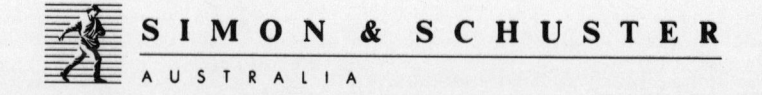

SIMON & SCHUSTER
AUSTRALIA

SIR DAVID MARTIN

First published in Australasia in 1996 by
Simon & Schuster Australia
20 Barcoo Street, East Roseville NSW 2069

Viacom International
Sydney New York London Toronto Tokyo Singapore

© Marea Stenmark 1996

All rights reserved. No part of this publication may be reproduced, stored in
a retrieval system or transmitted in any form or by any means, electronic, mechanical,
photocopying, recording or otherwise, without the prior permission of the publisher
in writing.

The Publishers would like to point out that every effort has been made to
acknowledge original source material and copyright holders of photographs included
in *Sir David Martin*. They would be pleased to hear from anyone who has not been
duly acknowledged.

National Library of Australia
Cataloguing-in-Publication data

Stenmark, Marea.
Sir David Martin: a man of courage and dedication.

Includes index.
ISBN 0 7318 0560 7.

1. Martin, David, Sir, 1933–1990. 2. Governors – New South
Wales – Biography. I. Title.

994.4063092

Designed by Megan Smith
Printed in Australia by Griffin Paperbacks

FOR LADY MARTIN
(Susie)
A woman of courage and dedication

Acknowledgements

Writing *Sir David Martin — A Man of Courage and Dedication* has been an illuminating experience. I have met, interviewed, listened to and learned from countless people who regarded it a pleasure to speak about Sir David Martin. Whether they knew him personally or by repute, everyone considered him a friend. I believe this was one of his greatest gifts. Instantly engaging, his crinkly smile and the twinkle in his eyes embraced us all.

I very much appreciate the important contribution many people have made to this book. I am indebted to them all.

The Rt. Hon. Sir Ninian Stephen KG, AK, GCMG, GCVO, KBE, honoured the book by writing the Foreword.

Lady Martin gave generously of her time and enthusiasm over the hours/days/weeks/months of remembrances, anecdotes and family stories. I felt privileged to be told them and given the authorisation to tell others through these pages. She also gave me access to an extensive collection of private papers and documents which have been treasured by the family for many years.

Sir David and Lady Martin's children — Sandy Di Pietro, Anna Beaumont and William Martin — met with me and sent faxes from England. Their frank opinions were welcome and refreshing.

Mrs Edna Little, Sir David's paternal aunt, generously provided me with precious letters and shared family secrets.

Margaret Hewlett, manuscript manager, has steered me through troubled waters — and muddy patches! — with sound advice, scheduling and unfailing good humour ... and hospitality.

Colin Bold has been a tower of strength. His knowledge, interest and involvement are very much appreciated. He also supplied a disk of Sir David's many speeches — a legacy indeed.

Wendy Barron, Manager, the Sir David Martin Foundation, provided photos and valuable information regarding this worthwhile organisation.

The Sebel of Sydney made the perfect venue for interviews in the intimacy of the Ricky May Lounge. Nicholas Truswell, General Manager — indeed, the entire Sebel staff — took a great interest in the project and were unfailingly courteous and supportive.

I contacted many people who had known David Martin in childhood, in youth, in the Navy or, in later times, at Government House. Unanimously they responded in giving freely of their time, advice and reminiscences. In strict alphabetical order (!), I acknowledge their support: Commodore Harold Adams AO, RAN (retired); Lieutenant Colin Bold RANR; Mrs W.M. Dempster; Mr Leo Duffy; Commander James Fahey AM, RAN (retired); Commander George Halley RAN (retired); Mr Bill Hunter; Mr Max Jagger (now deceased); Lieutenant Commander Ian Jagger RANR; Captain J.O. (Jo) Morrice RAN (retired); Mrs Sarah Renwick (née Adams); Commander Ken Swain AM, RAN (retired); Captain Norman Harold Stephen (Knocker) White RAN (retired).

Reginald Robertson's video, 'The Governor of New South Wales', was of great assistance. Reg himself was accommodating and enthusiastic throughout.

The Royal Australian Navy generously gave advice, photographs and a video of the RAN's Seventy-fifth Anniversary Celebration.

Alan Zammit, Naval historian, gave invaluable assistance through his writings, photographs and all-round help.

Louise Hawkins helped the research process by deciphering tapes. Noelene Donovan gave additional typing assistance.

Without the writings of Bert Weston, who recorded the family history, many valuable stories and facts would have been unavailable.

Radio 2UE kindly provided a tape from the Alan Jones breakfast program, which contained helpful statistics and facts.

Selwa Anthony, my friend, mentor and Author Management Agent to boot, has never wavered in her belief in this book or its author. At the end of all correspondence with Selwa, I sign 'YAGWSA', which is an abbreviation of, 'You're a good woman, Selwa Anthony'. She replies, 'TOTKOMS', which means, 'Takes one to know one, Marea Stenmark'!

My special appreciation to publishers Simon & Schuster Australia. I was most fortunate to have the following people assist and encourage me. Susan Morris-Yates first saw the book's potential. Jon Attenborough then attended a meeting with Selwa Anthony and myself, and within minutes we were all smiling. Brigitta Doyle, Senior Editor, could not have shown greater care, was infinitely patient, and never lost her eye for detail and quality. Or her sense of humour! Lynne Segal, Commissioning Editor, demonstrated her great experience and maturity. Karen Williams, Marketing Manager, brought zest and energy, plus her own brand of expertise. Julianne Sheedy, Publicist, kept me working ... and smiling. We were a happy team.

Without the encouragement and support of family and friends, I could never have completed this substantial task on time. I thank you all for understanding when I explained, 'Sorry ... can't come ... writing ...'!

Marea Stenmark OAM
Sydney, 1996

Contents

FOREWORD BY SIR NINIAN STEPHEN

FOR'ARD *1*

CHAPTER ONE ■ *The tender years 15*

CHAPTER TWO ■ *Lest we forget 28*

CHAPTER THREE ■ *The call of the sea 40*

CHAPTER FOUR ■ *A shipboard romance 48*

CHAPTER FIVE ■ *Ship spirit 58*

CHAPTER SIX ■ *From Torrens to Tresco 65*

CHAPTER SEVEN ■ *Seventy-fifth Anniversary Celebration 77*

CHAPTER EIGHT ■ *A short retirement 93*

CHAPTER NINE ■ *Father of the Year 101*

CHAPTER TEN ■ *Enter Government House 111*

CHAPTER ELEVEN ■ *Exit Government House 130*

CHAPTER TWELVE ■ *A fond farewell 136*

CHAPTER THIRTEEN ■ *The Sir David Martin Foundation 144*

AFT *151*

SOURCES *172*

INDEX *175*

Foreword

~

Life in Australia's Government House seldom offers scope for heroism. The Vice-Regal role is a very demanding one in terms of community service and much else as well, but rarely is more called for than a sensitive understanding of the demands of the office, coupled with a sense of duty and a determination to do that duty to the full.

In 1990, however, New South Wales provided a poignant exception; that exception was Sir David Martin. By 1990, Sir David had already achieved high success in one career of service to the nation and was embarked upon a second, which promised no less brilliance. He had given distinguished service as an outstanding Naval Commander in most active service at sea for many years and, later, ashore during four years as Flag Officer Naval Support Command in Sydney. Retiring as Rear Admiral, he had barely drawn breath in retirement when he accepted appointment as the thirty-fourth Governor of his native state of New South Wales.

Taking office in January 1989, he and Lady Martin served with distinction and great warmth in the Vice-Regal Office. Then, quite suddenly, in 1990, that most virulent cancer of the lungs, mesothelioma, long dormant, made its attack and it was very soon clear to him that death was near at hand. By the winter of 1990, he was thin, grey of face and pitifully short of breath, a supply of oxygen his constant companion.

The seventh of August, 1990, was Sir David's last day in office. In the manner of his leaving, the heroic quality of the man was manifest. First a short and moving farewell speech in Government House, delivered in full uniform and, through sheer willpower, without the benefit of oxygen; then a farewell word and a gift to each of the staff, a goodbye to the Premier and a royal salute taken, followed by a drive, for the last time, through the gates of Government House and, as it proved, for the last time, too, through the streets of Sydney, past Parliament and Courts.

All Australia saw that scene, either at first hand from the kerb or in the media nationwide, as he was driven, Lady Martin beside him, in an open car through streets lined with crowds. He used no oxygen, though a supply lay beside him. He sat erect, smiling and waving to the well-wishing crowd; they waved their greetings back, yet mourned his passing. He well knew, and they guessed, that this was to be his last sight of the city and its people, but all he did that day reflected his unfaltering courage and devotion to duty. That was when heroism touched the Vice-Regal Office.

The drive that day led him, that afternoon, to hospital where, three days later, he died, starved of breath.

This book now tells of David Martin's life of service to nation and State and is a fitting memorial to a very distinguished Australian.

The Rt. Hon. Sir Ninian Stephen KG, AK, GCMG, GCVO, KBE

For'ard

Some day I am sure George will marry me and we will have a family of many children

He was the first British Military Officer to land in Port Jackson, one of the discoverers of the River Hawkesbury and Lieutenant Governor of New South Wales.

She was a convict, a milliner, Jewish, and an unmarried mother whose child was born in Newgate Prison.

They were the great-great-great-grandparents of Sir David Martin.

A nation was born when George Johnston, in wig, red coat and white breeches, stepped ashore at Sydney Cove on 26 January 1788. He arrived on the back of a barefoot convict, James Ruse, who carried him through the shallows. It was the beginning of an extraordinary career; one which was shared by Esther Abrahams, who stole two cards of black lace, sailed to Australia in the same ship as George, bore him seven children and, twenty-five years later, became his wife.

Their backgrounds could not have been more different. The Johnstons were a powerful clan whose name, which can be found in records from the thirteenth century, was derived from the Barony of Johnston in Annandale, Scotland. The family crest, conferred by the King of Scotland, was a winged spur; their motto, *Nunquam non Paratus* (Always Ready).

George Johnston was born on 19 March 1764, the son of an officer who served in the American Revolution as aide-de-camp to Lord Percy, who later became Duke of Northumberland. George joined the army at the age of twelve and, under the patronage of the Duke, the Johnston family was able to purchase for him a commission as Second Lieutenant in the 45th Company of Marines in 1776.

For the next two years, the child officer served with his company in Nova Scotia and New York State and, in the battle at Bunker Hill, distinguished himself by saving the regimental flag from the hands of the dying ensign and bearing it to the front. He also served in the East and West Indies and, later, the coast of Africa. At the age of twenty-four, on his return to England, he volunteered for service in New South Wales and sailed with Captain Phillip in the First Fleet to form a settlement at Botany Bay on the east coast of Australia.

Esther Abrahams, on the other hand, entered a London shop on 27 July 1786 and stole two cards of silk lace from an open box on the counter. Obviously it was despair that drove her to the theft, for she was pregnant at fifteen. Despite the very good character references given by her three witnesses at her trial, she was sentenced to seven years, transportation, and her baby girl was born inside the walls of Newgate Gaol on 18 March 1787. It was some weeks before she joined the 102 women waiting aboard the passenger ship *Lady Penrhyn* for the voyage to Australia. Apart from the small crew and the marine guards, there were no other males on board — the entire list was comprised of female convicts.

When the First Fleet duly anchored at Botany Bay, they were disappointed to find themselves in a barren environment with little shelter from wind and weather, poor soil and very little prospect of success. Governor Phillip decided to look at the bay a few miles to the north, which Captain Cook had mentioned but not explored himself. So, on 21 January, a small group of boats entered Sydney Harbour for the first time.

Four years later, Esther Abrahams wrote to her mother:

Sydney Town,
Jan. 26, 1792

My Dearest Mother,

Never will I forget that sad day when you parted from me as they dragged me off to Newgate Prison where my little Rosanna was born. It was cruel to send me to seven years of long exile. What had I done but try to take a few yards of silk lace that Rosanna's father forced me to steal and I was only a girl of 15? Our parting nearly killed me.

It was a bitter thing to happen to a Jewish child and I am still ashamed that I have hurt the Abrahams name and all our family who have been good people in London. But nearly six years have passed since that day of our parting. I am a woman of 21 and I now have a little boy of two years who is called George Johnston after his father.

Rosanna is growing to be a fine girl and in this healthy climate she thrives like all the children born in New South Wales. I have never heard of her father Juliano again but if you see him do not tell him where I am. Some day I am sure that George will marry me and we will have a family of many children.

I met George when they put me aboard the *Lady Penrhyn* at Portsmouth to come to this country. He was a young officer of 23 and he has since become a captain of the marines. Mother, he has been a great comfort to me and without him I cannot tell what would have become of Rosanna and me. George often says that I was the most beautiful girl he ever saw, with my black hair hanging below my shoulders, my oval face and almond eyes and many have said the same since and think me the beauty of Botany Bay.

On the *Lady Penrhyn* I was thin and nearly naked in the rags they gave us to wear but Captain Phillip was kind and good and got better clothes for us. The voyage took so long but they gave us enough to eat and I could feed my baby. George protected me from the marines who had their way with some of the other girls. There were no fallen girls among us but many of us since our arrival here have had to live with the men and some have married.

In the first two years we nearly starved and we thought how cruel they were at home to send us here and leave us without food for so long. The worst thing was to be without tea and we had no salt or sugar ... I could not keep up my milk for Rosanna and had to feed her my rations as she would have died without them.

When we arrived at Botany Bay, George told me that the officers thought that Captain Cook and the men with him must have been silly to say it was a good place to make a Settlement. The worst thing was that Captain Phillip could not find water at Botany Bay. Even here at Sydney Cove the soil grows so little but we hope to be better off soon because a man called Ruse has begun to tend maize and wheat up the river at Parramatta. George is trying to get some land and we hope that he will be given 100 acres at Petersham. George wants to call it Annandale Farm after the place where he was born in Scotland.

Do not worry about me, Mother, because this will be a good land for George and me and our children to live in and Rosanna will find a good husband when she grows up. Tell grandfather that I am happy and still try to worship the God of Abraham, Isaac and Jacob in the prayers that he taught me. There are a few Jews here but George is a Christian and had little George baptised. The Chaplain is a kindly man. I will ask him to visit you when he goes home.

The voyage was a dreadful experience for Esther Abrahams. It is little wonder that she was glad to accept whatever help and protection were available to her by becoming the mistress of Lieutenant Johnston, now Captain Johnston, who was handsome, ambitious and, despite being in his early twenties, a veteran of years of colonial warfare. Very soon Esther was expecting her second child.

The child was a son, and they gave him his father's name. He was baptised on 4 March 1790 as 'Abrahams or Johnston, George, son of George Johnston, Captain Lieutenant of Marines and Esther Abrahams, convict'. Two days later, George left Sydney for the first convict settlement on Norfolk Island, accompanied by Esther and his son. Her daughter Rosanna was left with a foster parent in Sydney.

George stayed on Norfolk Island for almost a year. He returned to Sydney in February 1791, and Esther and young George followed him in May. On 9 March 1792, she gave birth to her second son, Robert, who later became the first Australian officer in the Royal Navy. His godfather was Governor Arthur Phillip. Robert Johnston was the only child honoured thus. Also, in 1792, when the time came for the Royal Marine Detachment to return to England, George was one of those who elected to stay behind and Phillip chose him as 'the most deserving marine officer to raise and command a company of marines and locals to be part of the New South Wales Corps'.

In February 1793, Esther's seven-year sentence expired and George received one of the 100-acre grants of land bestowed upon the officers of the first garrison. The piece of land he chose was 4 miles along the road from Sydney to Parramatta, and, eventually, was increased to 390 acres. He named it Annandale, after his birthplace. The Duke of Northumberland sent gifts of a stallion, a ram and several ewes to establish their farm. No doubt he and Esther made many plans for the development of Annandale, but at that time he was still engaged in his duties as King's officer.

In 1796, George Johnston was sent to Norfolk Island again, taking his son George, now six, with him. Esther remained behind to supervise Annandale, and in 1799 the family moved in to the fine home they had built on the estate. Their house was made of brick, one of few such buildings in the colony at that time. It was large, spacious, single-storeyed and surrounded by the wide, shady verandahs that became the distinctive style of Australian home architecture.

It was not long before Annandale became self-contained. It had its own slaughterhouse, butchery, bakery, blacksmith's shop and stores, and the orange grove and vineyards they had planted were thriving. They also planted a magnificent avenue of Norfolk Island pines which George had brought back with him. They were the first to be brought into New South Wales. As an indication of George's status, in 1800 they had sixteen convicts assigned to them as servants and labourers — one of the largest allocations in the colony.

In 1800, the third child of George Johnston and Esther Abrahams, David, was born. During the next ten years they had four more children, all girls: Maria in 1801, Julia in 1803, Isabella in 1804 (who died in 1806) and Blanche in 1809, who died in August 1904 at the age of ninety-five.

At Governor Phillip's suggestion, George had transferred from the Royal Marines and become an officer in the New South Wales Corps. This regiment had been formed specially for service in the penal colony, but it rapidly gained monopoly over trade, particularly over rum, earning it the infamous title of 'Rum Corps'. By 1794, Captain William Paterson was Commander of the Corps. Under his leadership, the men were encouraged to engage in trading ventures and land allocations. There was little discipline, and quarrels and disputes over profits were common. Following one such quarrel between Paterson and George, Paterson ordered George's arrest on charges of 'paying spirits to a serjeant [sic] as part of his pay at an improper price, contempt, and disobedience or orders'.

George was sent to England for trial, sailing on HMS *Buffalo* in October 1800. He took eight-year-old Robert with him, believing it was time for him to go to an English boarding school. Once in England, the London authorities saw that it was no mere disciplinary matter, and found that George could not be tried by the English courts. In 1802, he was returned to Sydney, where he and Paterson resolved their differences and the case was dropped.

As the proportion of Irish convicts in the colony rose, so did their desire for more power, and in March 1804 an uprising took place which became known as the Castle Hill Rebellion. George Johnston had replaced William Paterson as Commander of the New South

Wales Corps and when Governor King proclaimed martial law, George played a large part in arresting the leaders of the rebellion and routing the rest of the rebels at Vinegar Hill, now known as Rouse Hill. For this service to the colony he was granted 2000 acres in the Cabramatta district.

Captain William Bligh was appointed to replace King as Governor of New South Wales in 1806. Bligh had survived the mutiny on his ship *Bounty* in 1789 and was a determined, harsh and arrogant man who rapidly fell foul of the self-made aristocracy of the colony. He had tried to suppress the rum trade controlled by the Corps in order to allow the smaller settlers an easier market for their produce and made enemies of the officers and those powerful in the colony. When he threatened to cancel the 5 000-acre grant of land made to John Macarthur, the wealthiest and most powerful colonist, and to disband or withdraw the New South Wales Corps, George Johnston took action.

On 26 January 1808, George, as the officer commanding the New South Wales Corps, received the following letter, signed by many of the colony's leading gentlemen:

> Sir — The present alarming state of this colony, in which every man's property, liberty, and life, are endangered, induces us most earnestly to implore you to place the Governor Bligh under arrest, and to assume the command of the colony. We pledge ourselves, at the moment of less agitation, to come forward to support the measure with our fortune and our lives.

After weighing the serious step he had been urged to take, George decided to act, and ordered the regiment to form in Barrack Square. Mounting his horse, with bands playing and colours flying, he marched on Government House and surrounded the building with soldiers. Lieutenant Minchin was sent forward with a letter addressed to 'William Bligh, Esq., F.R.S., etc.' in which he was informed by Major Johnston that, 'being charged by the respectable inhabitants with crime that render you unfit to exercise the supreme authority another moment in the colony', he was required to resign his authority and submit to arrest, under which he was placed 'by the advice of every respectable inhabitant in the town of Sydney'. The letter was signed by George Johnston as Acting Lieutenant-Governor and Major commanding the New South Wales Corps. Governor Bligh, who, it is said, was found concealed under a bed and covered with dust, was brought under guard before Major Johnston, who formally placed him under arrest, and thenceforth, for eight months, took command of the colony.

Bligh was kept prisoner in Government House for more than a year, until Lieutenant-Colonel Joseph Foveaux arrived on his way to take command of Norfolk Island and, as the senior officer, took over the administration of New South Wales. Foveaux was succeeded by Paterson, who had returned from Van Diemen's Land, and on 23 March 1808, George was given full military honours when he embarked for England and a court-martial for his part in the revolt against Bligh. He returned to England in the same ship as Bligh which couldn't have been easy for either of them! The court-martial, held in May 1811, found him guilty of mutiny. A military offence such as this could have been punished by death, but the officers of the court were sympathetic towards George and recognised, tacitly at least, that despite his arrest of Bligh, he had not engineered any plot or challenged the rule of law and order. He was cashiered from the army — a very mild sentence — and permitted to return to New South Wales as a 'free settler' in continued enjoyment of the 7 000 acres of land which by this time had been granted to him by the Crown.

Immediately after George's departure for his court-martial in 1808, Esther had made a hasty application for a grant of land. On 30 June 1809, Lieutenant-Governor William Paterson granted her 570 acres on the Georges River near Bankstown, adjoining a farm owned already by George Johnston.

Whatever peace of mind she was given by Paterson's grant of land, however, was short-lived. Late in 1809, Colonel Lachlan Macquarie, accompanied by 700 men of the 73rd Regiment, arrived in Sydney as the new Governor and began as he meant to continue — by reorganising the New South Wales Corps. It was the beginning of a soberly progressive era in which political power was taken firmly out of military and into administrative hands, and a by-product of the process was a cancellation of all grants and leases made between Bligh's arrest and Governor Macquarie's arrival. On 10 October 1810, Esther begged for confirmation of her land grant from the new Governor, emphasising that she had a large family, and that it was her intention to settle in the country.

Her appeal failed to move Governor Macquarie. In his handwriting, the petition shows his judgement: 'inadmissable'. Esther, however, literally stood her ground and continued to live on the property until 1813, when George returned to Australia from the court-martial in England. Once George was in Australia, Governor Macquarie decided that he was 'a fine fellow'. Esther was allowed legal ownership of the land with the grant unconditionally confirmed. The register of original grants in the Bankstown parish map shows 'Esther Julian' as grantee of 570 acres.

The friendship between George Johnston and Governor Macquarie took another unexpected turn. Feeling that George should not remain the father of 'seven little Australians' who were illegitimate offspring, the Governor urged and persuaded him to rectify the situation. The marriage register of the Church of St John's, Parramatta, shows that on 12 November 1814, 'George Johnston of Annandale married Mrs Esther Julian of the same place'. The wedding took place at Concord, twenty-five years after the couple had arrived in Sydney with the First Fleet. It was celebrated by Samuel Marsden, and one of the witnesses was Esther's firstborn child, Rosanna!

George's success as a farmer and his love of the land had earned him great respect and affection. He was the first to introduce clover into the Illawarra district. From the early days of the colony, he had played a variety of important roles and had been the central character in many stirring scenes.

On 19 February 1820, George Johnston junior, Esther and George's eldest child, was killed in a horse race through the bush whilst mustering. He was among Australia's first and finest daredevil riders and stockmen. Governor Macquarie told the grief-stricken parents: 'Your son was an honour to his name, his family, and the country that God gave him birth, of which he was one of the brightest ornaments'.

Three years after his son's death, on 5 January 1823, George Johnston died 'after a short but severe illness'. He was fifty-eight. He left to 'the mother of his children ... for the term of her natural life the estate of Annandale'. Robert was to succeed Esther in this inheritance, whilst David received the Georges River estate — appropriately named George's Hall — where he became a leading grazier.

Robert resented the fact that Annandale was left to his mother's care. He asked the court to declare Esther insane and, less than a week later, the inquiry opened. Esther engaged David Poole as solicitor in her defence. He had to face W.C. Wentworth, a member of the famous family which is still prominent in Australian law and politics today.

The principal witness for Robert's application was the physician Dr William Bland, who described Esther as eccentric, quick-tempered and of a brusque manner. He added he had seen her frantically driving through the streets and that she should be placed under personal restraint. Even David Poole admitted that Esther had strange habits, heightened by her occasional practice of drinking too freely.

Esther's only witness was Jacob Isaacs, who owned a public house and 50 acres of cleared land at Petersham, on the Parramatta Road. He told how Esther had frequently sought refuge in his home, wanting protection from her son Robert, complaining about his behaviour, and showing Isaacs her bruises from Robert's acts of violence. Isaacs testified that she had accumulated her property by hard struggle, that he had seen her superintending the concerns of the farm and considered her a woman fully capable of minding her own affairs.

Wentworth called two of Robert's assigned servants to the witness box, and even Esther's grandson, Charles Nichols (Rosanna's child), to give evidence against her.

Sensing that his case was not going well, Poole requested an adjournment so that more witnesses might be called, but Wentworth pressed for a decision. The jury retired for a very short time — one hour — returning with the finding that Mrs Esther Johnston, although she had lucid intervals, was 'not of sound mind, nor capable of managing her affairs'. Trustees were appointed for the estate. Robert was not declared the heir at law.

Esther lived for another fifteen years, most of them on her son David's estate. When she died, on 26 August 1846, Robert obeyed the instructions in his father's will that she be buried in the family vault at Annandale, designed by one of the colony's most renowned architects, Francis Greenaway. She lay there, undisturbed, for many years, until Annandale was subdivided and a new vault was built at Waverley Cemetery. Today she rests there by her husband's side, described as 'Esther the relict', above the Pacific, just before it bends towards Port Jackson, where their ship so fatefully entered in 1788.

CHAPTER ONE

The Tender Years

I hope you'll be back soon, I've been looking after Mummy for you.

With such an illustrious ancestry, it is hardly surprising that David Martin was imbued with many of the qualities of Esther and George: dedication, courage, strength of spirit and a great love of Australia.

If things had gone according to plan, David would have been born in Capetown, where his father, a Naval officer, had been on exchange with the fledgling South African Navy. Instead, Commander William Harold Martin, known to all as Bill, was transferred to New South Wales and was on terra firma at the time.

The early hours of 15 April 1933 found Bill running up and down the streets of Sydney's Eastern Suburbs, urgently calling for a taxi to take his wife, now in advanced stages of labour, to hospital. They arrived at Denholm Private Hospital, Darling Point, just in time, for David James Martin was born shortly after. 'Yellow as saffron' is the description given by his paternal aunt, Mrs Edna Little, who, at ninety-five, recalls the occasion as if it were yesterday.

David was christened in his parents' house and was well behaved during the ceremony. He was a beautiful little boy — blue-eyed, with golden curls, always contented and a lover of his food. The only time he used to cry was when the meal was finished, then 'tears like pear drops ran down his cheeks'. At the age of two or three he was quite a shy lad who didn't like to be made a fuss of; he had 'a lovely spirit', was communicative and charming and given to quaint comments.

The Martins were a close-knit unit of three. His mother, Isla Estelle, who disliked her name and was always known as Jim, and father, Bill, made sure that David was an unspoiled child. They had many friends, both in Australia and overseas, and relatives in South Australia and country towns as well. They had simple holidays together — there wasn't a great deal of money, but they had everything they wanted in their little world. Water was their love — they always lived near it and often went sailing.

Commander William Martin was away at sea for long periods of time, during which David and his mother formed a great friendship. He was naturally well mannered, and Jim ensured that he was disciplined, kind and patient. She realised that he was precocious and that his intelligence and keen sense of humour had to be exercised well. When his father was home on leave, the place came alive. Like most Naval men, Bill put a huge effort into being a husband and father during the periods he was ashore. He was a happy, enthusiastic, energetic man with a zest for living and a great sense of fun. Together he and David would run down to the beach at Double Bay in the very early morning, then go around the back of the baker's shop on the way home to collect a loaf of bread as it came out of the oven. He was always the life of the party, loved all sports and would 'dress up' at the drop of a hat, don a fake moustache and strum on a ukulele.

When the time came for Bill to go back to sea, Jim and David would pick up the threads of their day-to-day lives once more. She to writing to her husband, who was also an avid correspondent, whilst David would experiment with his latest words. When still quite a young boy, he wrote to his Aunt Edna thanking her for sending him some money to see a theatrical show: 'If I don't join the Navy [a foregone conclusion] then I shall *indubitably* be an actor!' He very much enjoyed theatre and the arts, knew every word of Gilbert & Sullivan operettas and, like his father, was always prepared to don an outfit for an occasion. Despite the age difference, he always called his relatives by their first names. When his mother pointed out that they may find this disrespectful and that perhaps he should address them as Aunt and Uncle he replied, 'I can't, they're my friends'. So it was always 'Ed' rather than 'Aunt' and 'Roy' instead of 'Uncle'.

David Martin's education began at Glamorgan School in Victoria, then, in 1940, when he was seven years old, he began attending The Scots College at Bellevue Hill in Sydney, where he entered Year 2, Class A. There he met Bill Hunter, and a friendship began which lasted a lifetime. Bill was from the country. His mother had taken a flat near the College, only 200 metres from where the Martins lived. Together the boys would walk home from school, and Jim would give them delicious hot bread rolls with banana filling for afternoon tea.

Bill, the boy from the bush, loved going to the Martins' home because David had good-quality English toys, brought back to Australia when he was very young. The Martins had been round the world, lived in many homes and collected artifacts from several countries. Bill's favourite was a blow pipe, in which he imagined there were poisoned darts!

The two boys would spend endless hours playing with David's train set and farm toys. They would divide up the farm sets then use monopoly money to trade. Bill bought all the stock, David ended up with all the money! They also built a cubby house and would play under the branches of the cumquat tree in the back garden. At other times they would make up three-act plays and perform for Jim's visitors, including her mother, Mrs Murray, a tall, grey-haired, kind but remote lady. David would perform the first act. Bill, who confesses he didn't have an acting bone in his body, would 'lumber through' the second act and David would do the third. But, best of all, David had a bike. He would 'double' Bill to Double Bay — it was a great adventure to go right to the top of the hill near Cooper Park and feel the thrill as they free-wheeled all the way down Bellevue Road. At other times they would go to Watsons Bay on the tram, hop off before the conductor collected the fare and wait for another. The only trouble was that the trams ran at half-hourly intervals and it would take them forever to get there! And all to buy a penny fudge which was made of water — the real McCoy was made with milk and cost the princely sum of threepence.

David was a self-sufficient child. He didn't miss having brothers and sisters. He was imaginative, loved sport, enjoyed school, and had good friends. During school holidays he went to stay at the Hunters' property, which was 90 kilometres north-west of Moree and 35 kilometres from a little town called Garah. Bill's father had been in World War I and had done his training at Mena Camp in Cairo before he went to Gallipoli. As a returned serviceman he was entitled to a settlement of land, and he called the property 'Mena' in memory of his experience at the training camp.

When at Mena, Bill and David spent their time riding ponies — Fury was David's horse — and David became a pretty good rider for a city slicker. They chased wild pigs, caught sucking pigs, chased kangaroos but never caught any, and collected emu eggs. They occasionally took their ponies to horse gymkhanas, riding 20 kilometres in the morning, then they'd gallop all day and usually stay overnight with friends before riding home the next day.

The early 1940s were hard years. There was constant drought and everything was rationed. Bill and David would feed the sheep. This was done by horse and dray because fuel was rationed. It was a slow and drawn-out exercise — Bill's father drove the draught horse and dray, David and Bill trailed corn behind. The sheep would follow along, eating the corn. They also had poddy lambs and chooks to feed, their own eggs and home-grown vegetables. They went to town only once a month and saved the petrol to do the shearing instead.

There were many such holidays at Mena. During one, David contracted measles and, because he was infectious, could not return to school with Bill. Mrs Hunter found him no trouble at all, describing him as 'the most beautiful boy I have ever seen. He was always well mannered, the perfect guest.'

The trips to Mena for the school holidays on the train — the North West Mail — were enormous fun. The carriages were always choc-a-block, with many passengers sleeping in corridors. In the middle of the night — this was the best part — Noel Williams, who went to Farrar Agricultural School at Tamworth, would join the train at Werris Creek then 'we'd bunk down outside the gents' loo on a couple of rugs and, as other kids got off, we'd get seats together', Bill recalls. It was after one of their trips home from Mena that they noticed there were dents in the road at Rose Bay and pieces of shrapnel were found on the oval at Scots College. Little did they realise then the true significance of their observations: whilst they were at Mena, Rose Bay had been shelled by Japanese submarines in May 1942. The shelling had occurred during the night they were on the train returning to Sydney after the holidays.

As well as having real friends, David had a very special imaginary friend, Hamish, who often wrote to Jim. As David himself was a great letter writer, his days were filled to overflowing, not only with outdoor activities but indoors too, with pencil and paper working overtime.

> Dear Jin
>
> I have ben sent to queensland and i will stay here for three munths. I an haveing a happy time. I have joynd the navy. I an going on bord H.M.A.S. Moresby when the three munths are up. I have a very light breakfast. I have found a girl freand her name is shela child. a freand of yours and Davids. David wants to Marry her.
>
> love from hameish

These were followed by other epistles, signed by David, ranging from enquiries regarding 'escrais' in 'hosbidal', descriptions of 'korker' times, 'busters' and even a request from Burrawang for his ration book to be sent to him. All his greetings were varied and full of love and fun. He addressed his mother in many forms: Mummy, Mum, Mother Hubbard, Mum Herring, 'Ahoy there cobber' and Jim. He signed himself as 'little fish', 'little peanut' and 'David', written in a variety of shapes and sizes.

>
> Mina
> Garah
> N.S.W. Sunday
>
> "Ahoy Ahoy there, cobber.
> I am very well and we had a nice trip up.
> Going to Mina from Garah we got
> flogged and had to get someone to pull
> us out. The sports went well; Bill won
> 7 bob and a ribbon but poor me won
> nothing. Fury & Rex are well. We
> moved the thingimyjigs today and they are
> going strong.
> Oh Well I must leave you now and
> write to Chris. Keep your chin up.
> David.

Dear Jim

I am so sorry I did not write on Friday or Monday but I have been too busy in the paddocks. Mrs Hunter makes us do nearly all the housework and make our beds. The Boomi Sports went well. I went in these following events:-

    Best Boy Rider (under 10)
    "   "   " under 15
    Best Pony Hack (ridden by boy or girl under 15)
    Musical Chairs
    Walk, Trot and Gallop
    Foot Race (won by Bill)

At the end a man let a little pig go on the ground for everybody to catch. One boy caught it by the head and a man reckoned the boy took it from him so the man grabbed it by the hind legs and the poor little piggy wiggy went 'eek eek eek!'. Bill and I are going out to see someone today and are looking forward to it. Hoping to see your fat face again.

David

As Christmas 1940 passed and New Year 1941 began, his father sent David a sketch of HMAS *Moresby* and, on 8 February 1942, just three days after joining HMAS *Perth*, he wrote describing 'what a fine ship this is'.

My Dear David,

Mummy will have told you how we had to do all my packing in a hurry. It was a pity as I had hoped to see quite a lot of Mummy while she was down. I hope you looked after Cynthia very well and that you and the dogs behaved yourselves.

I believe you have taken a lot of my fancy dress gear. If you look after it as I have done it will last you for a long time and you'll have lots of fun with it.

You have been on board once or twice and know what a fine ship this is. Next time I come home I'll ask you on board again and you can see my cabins. They're not as big as Captain Wallers but they are very nice ones.

I hope you will keep up your swimming while I am away. I think it would be a good idea if you went swimming with the school this term. And I hope that this term you will try very hard with your arithmetic. I think you can do very well if you try. I haven't time to write any more now. You are the man of the house and must look after Mummy and Cynthia and do all you can to help. Tell Mummy she can give you 6d a week for me if you deserve it.

With love from
Daddy

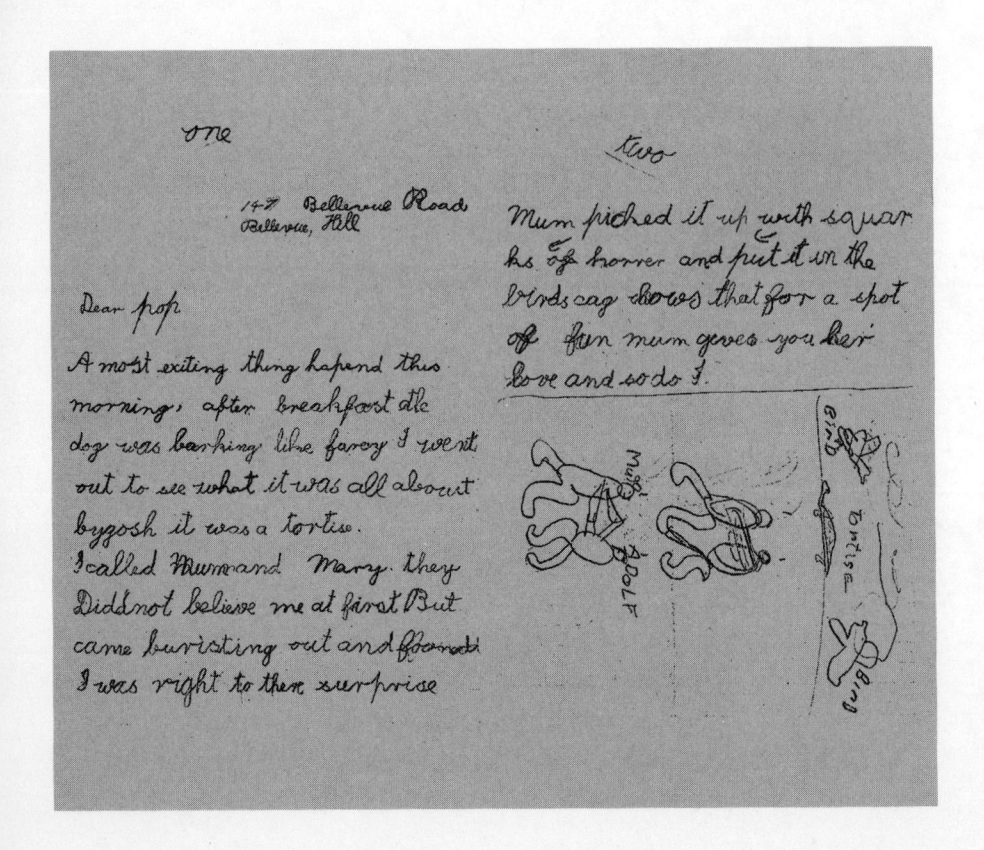

one

14 Bellevue Road
Bellevue, Hill

Dear pop,
A most exiting thing hapend this morning, after breakfast the dog was barking like farcy I went out to see what it was all about bygosh it was a tortis.
I called Mum and Mary. they Did not believe me at first But came buristing out and found I was right to ther surprise

two

Mum picked it up with squar ks of horror and put it in the birdscag shows that for a spot of fun mum geves you her love and so do I.

David never failed to return his father's correspondence, enthusiastically describing in great detail and with full illustrations the antics of the dogs and a 'tortise'. He even added a coin, stuck on to the back of one letter, with the notation 'hears [sic] one of my 3d from the pudding for you for luck'. He was a generous, sharing little boy who signed his letters 'your beloved son, David'. In another letter he sent his father a map of Australia, on which he'd drawn welcoming faces preparing for his father's return home.

On 13 March 1942, a bright pink 'Urgent Telegram' arrived, and the lives of David and Jim were changed. Irrevocably.

> With deepest regret I have to inform you your husband Commander William Harold Martin RAN is missing as a result of enemy action STOP Minister and Navy and the Naval Boar [sic] desire to express to you their sincere sympathy

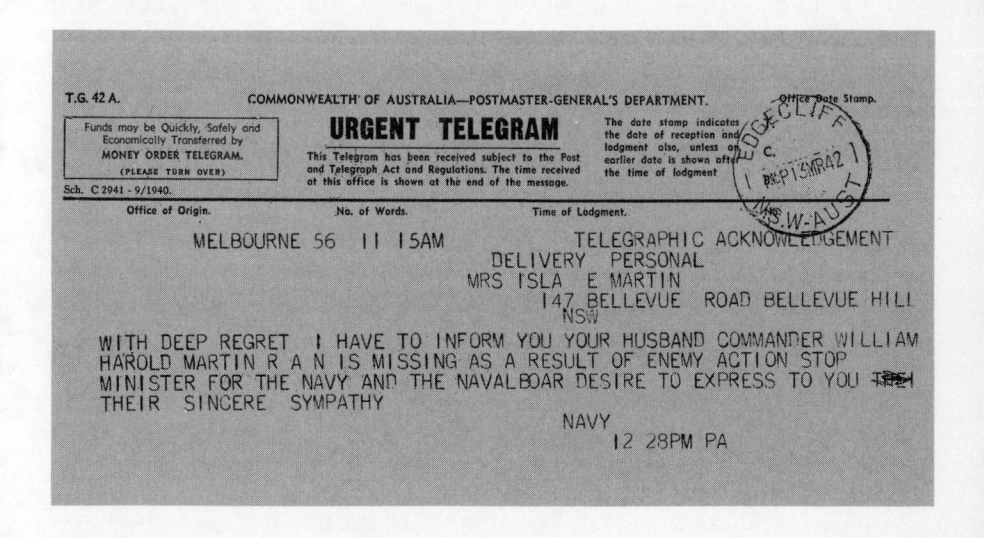

Missing. Only missing. There was still hope. This was a time for keeping busy; usual things had to be done. David knew he must help his mother and succeed at school. He did both, and it appeared to his classmates that he was 'just a regular kid'.

However, the news and subsequent uncertainty about his father did affect David, for it was about this time that he developed a mild stutter. With the Navy still as his dream, he knew that he would not be accepted unless he conquered it. Jim sent him to a speech therapist for many months at great expense and, at the end of it all, he emerged with clear speech. He had also acquired a great love of the classics, prompted by reading aloud from the tomes he was given by his teacher. During this time, Jim also read aloud so that David would become used to the sound of voices in the house. With only two of them, the place seemed strangely silent.

David's principal at Scots Prep, Mr R.G. Edyvene, made a great impression and was a strong influence on David as a young boy. David emulated his phrases and a love of the English language was fostered in him. The boys at school would listen to Churchill's speeches and collectively and fervently vow 'We will never give in'.

David became a weekly boarder at the College in the early 1940s, and Jim took up a position as Assistant Bursar there. Both attacked their respective roles with determination and courage, and David's school reports were exemplary. In Term 1 of 1942, David came top in composition, reading, poetry, spelling and dictation, but he dropped to twelfth position in tables and seventh in arithmetic. His Term 2 report states that 'he is a well mannered boy, always a pleasure to teach', 'his football is not impressive', his spelling and dictation 'consistently excellent'. With thirty-seven boys now in the form, David's Term 2 report confirmed his top place in several subjects, but in arithmetic he came … eleventh!

The remarks from the Principal and Master in Charge between 1942 and 1945 were invariably complimentary: 'Quiet, well mannered and altogether a most promising boy … he will be a power in the school in days to come'; 'A boy of character with easy manners and the right attitude towards his work, though a little inclined to talk out of turn'; 'He has both balance and charm of manner which will stand by him through life'; 'A boy of courage and determination whose efforts have all been directed into the right channels'; 'He has both intelligence and a sense of humour. His future prospects are bright'; 'David is imbued with competitive spirit and will not turn out any work of inferior quality; altogether he impresses most favourably'.

It was not until 31 January 1946, almost four years after the urgent telegram, that Jim received the following letter from the Commonwealth of Australia:

Dear Madam,

Since the termination of hostilities in August, 1945, an exhaustive investigation, which included enquiries made from repatriated Prisoners of War, has been conducted in an effort to obtain news of personnel who were missing as the result of the sinking of H.M.A.S. PERTH.
 This investigation has now been completed and it is with deep regret I have to inform you that no hope can now be held that your husband, Commander William Harold Martin, R.A.N., is still alive.
 The evidence reveals that, when the order to abandon ship was given, your husband was known to have set out to escape. Unfortunately no evidence was forthcoming that he succeeded in reaching land. It is believed that many were killed by underwater explosions immediately prior to sinking of H.M.A.S. PERTH.
 The Naval Board have, therefore, reluctantly concluded that the death of your husband occurred on or after 1st March, 1942, and have accepted this date for official purposes.
 The Minister for the Navy and the Naval Board can fully realise the grief this sad news will bring after many anxious months of waiting, and they desire me again to convey to you their sincere sympathy.

Seven months later, another letter, dated 23 August 1946, confirmed the worst. It stated that it had come to the notice of the Naval Board that some relatives still held hopes that additional personnel from the ship were alive. Accordingly they detailed a ship of the Royal Australian Navy to make a further search of the islands and mainland in the vicinity of the Sunda Strait where *Perth* was sunk. The letter concluded by saying 'the search has now been completed and I regret to inform you the result has furnished no information which could give any hope that there are more survivors'.

During the years since his father had disappeared, David had never given up hope that he was still alive, somewhere. David later said, 'I felt sure he'd come back again'. He had continued to write to him, keeping his father informed of the happenings at home and school. Written in ink (gone was the pencil), this last letter, dated 23 August 1945, showed maturity way beyond his twelve years.

Dear Daddy,

(Please excuse the pansy ink). I hope you are quite well. We have been keeping the house and garden in order while you have been away, both tedious jobs; but still, to get back to the subject: I am writing from home on a lovely new writing table. I am still at 'Scots' and this is my last year at the prep. I am in the third fifteen and third eleven, and this year I hope to make the athletic team. This year I sit for the scholarship, next year I sit for the Naval College Exam. At present I am in form 6a at the prep and hope to get a good form position. In football I play front-row forward, and our team came through the season unbeaten. I am sorry we haven't any photographs to send you for I'm sure you wont recognise me, mummy says I've grown easily six feet and I can lift her up now. I am a weekly boarder now and we have great fun in the dormitories pillow-fighting etc. I am very keen on Edna and Roy, Edna's a dear, and I like Roy very much. I will be going up to stay with them when they settle down at the farm. I have been spending most of my holidays at Moree with a boy named Bill

Hunter. I go to church on Sundays at H.M.A.S. 'Rushcutter' with the Newcombs. It's great fun down there. I'm itching to see you after three and a half years. I hope you'll be back soon, I've been looking after mummy for you.

Love from David

Although still only a boy, David's goals were clearly defined: look after his mother now that he was officially the man of the house; succeed at Scots; and follow his father's footsteps to a career in the Navy.

CHAPTER TWO

LEST WE FORGET

Teach David to be proud of the memory and work of his father

In the months and years that followed these events, Jim had many lonely times. David was away as a weekly boarder, she worked hard during the day, and the nights were filled with memories. She had sustained a mixture of grief and uncertainty. The prolonged anxiety of not knowing if her husband were alive or dead had been heightened by financial hardship. She had not received any of Bill's salary — the Navy had ceased payment — from the time of the sinking of *Perth* until the official notification of his death, whereupon his accumulated deferred pay was made over to her. She had endured years of loneliness, years of wondering, and was now shattered by the certain knowledge that Bill was dead.

Jim and Bill had met in the near East on board a liner. She was seventeen, he was twenty-five. A slip of a girl, she had been attracted to his outgoing personality, warmth and charm, but most of all his loving nature. Bill was a very popular, happy character — always ready for whatever lay ahead. As a teenager he had been of average height and had feared that he wouldn't be tall enough for the Navy. When asked at the interview, 'What do you think you could do in the Navy?' he replied with customary optimism: 'I could rise to be an Admiral'. They were a classic example of opposites attracting. He so full of life, capable and resourceful, she so quiet, dignified, reserved and unable to boil water. The eight year difference in their ages didn't seem to matter at all. She was well read, could discuss anything, loved gardens and flowers and things of beauty.

Bill had always been very protective of Jim and often referred to her as 'my darlingest small child'. In a letter written whilst in the Johore Strait, he began 'My darling, darling, James', and concluded with:

> I hope I'll never disappoint you darling, or cause you any pain at all. My object in life is to go on loving you and trying to make you happy. If I can succeed in that I'll have done well.
>
> Heavens dear, but you have made a difference to me. The very thought of not being with you makes me feel sick.

She re-read his letters often and kept them, along with other precious papers, tied together with ribbon. In this bundle was a press clipping from 1916, when Bill had been one of twenty-five young men selected for entry to the Royal Australian Naval College as Cadet Midshipmen. There was also a list of ships on which he had served, from HMAS *Encounter* in 1920 to *Perth* in 1942, and a special letter to Jim's mother in Singapore (where the Murrays had disembarked) in which he had made a request: 'I would like to know if I find favour in your eyes as a prospective son-in-law'. He did.

> Labuan
> 23rd July 1929
>
> Dear Mrs. Murray,
>
> During the past year I've thought and thought about this letter and each time I've decided against writing it. I can't resist any longer as I'm afraid that the heat of Singapore may be too much for you and that you may leave before I see you and James.
>
> I love your James and want to marry her. I hope that she feels the same way about me. I wanted to tell her so in the

'Arafina' and I jolly nearly did on that last day when you sailed. In all fairness I couldn't as, after all, she was only seventeen, had only known me for three weeks and we were not going to see each other for two years. In any case I had very little to offer.

I think I explained my financial position to you in the 'Arafina'. I have about £200 to my name and my pay and I have no 'expectations' apart from rises of pay — which, at the moment, is £440 a year. In two years time it should be £570. At the end of 1932 I'd be getting nearly £700 a year. I think my position in the Service is fairly sound and if I don't make a fool of myself I should get as far as Commander. We can discuss all this when we meet but I would like to know if I find favour in your eyes as a prospective son in law.

I hate to try and imagine a life without James in it and I'm praying that I have your approval and good wishes.

I don't intend saying anything to James until I see her and she sees me. She mightn't like me at all when she sees me again. I can't imagine my own feelings changing at all but then I'm a few years older than she is.

I try to be optimistic about the time we'll get to Singapore but I don't really think there's a hope of us getting there before about 20th August. Getting leave while on the Surveying Ground is an almost unheard of thing and I don't think I'll get mine.

My only hope is that you won't leave Singapore before we get there.

Please Mrs Murray, have I your approval and permission to carry on hoping? I know how much you love James and understand her and I don't want to do anything without your approval.

Be careful of your health in Singapore. It's very hot in August and July and we dare not take risks.

Yours affectionately
Bill

They were married on Wednesday, 15 January 1930, when Jim was nineteen. It was an elegant Naval wedding at St Stephen's Church, Sydney, and the reception was held at fashionable Ushers Hotel, where they smiled for the social pages as they cut the cake, fashioned in the shape of a warship. David was born three years later, and the ensuing years had been happy and busy, with time spent in England and Australia. Now, widowed at thirty-two, life was very different.

There were still more letters to be absorbed: to his mother, written from Fort William and Edinburgh in July 1936 when the threesome had a holiday in Scotland, from London in August and, the following year, 12 May 1937, several tightly typed pages devoted to the Coronation. Then came a Roll of Honour in the *Sydney Morning Herald,* which included Bill's name, listing those 'previously reported missing, now believed lost in Sunda Straits'.

Lastly, there was a letter of sympathy, which meant a great deal to Jim, from J.A. Edgell. A famous Royal Navy Hydrographer of Rear Admiral rank, he regarded Bill as 'the coming man in the Hydrographic Branch', believing him to be a chart maker of distinction in the science of measuring and describing seas, lakes and rivers.

> 13 October 1942
>
> My Dear Jim,
>
> I have only today heard that your husband was serving in the 'Perth' during the fighting off Java and that he is reported as missing and presumed to have gone down with the ship.
> The news was a terrible shock to me because I thought he was in the 'Moresby', or at all events engaged on surveying work.
> There is so little that one can say and nothing at all that can bring solace or comfort to you.
> You know of course that I was very fond of your husband and that I regarded him as the coming man in the Hydro-

graphic Branch and one who would go far and achieve much distinction.

I do not like favourites and have always avoided taking more interest in one officer than another; but I know that W.H. Martin *was* my favourite officer in the 'Moresby' and I have watched his progress ever since.

His pride in his profession and in you and David were alike immense and I am sure that he gave himself completely in performing the duties of Commander of the 'Perth'. It was like him to take up such an appointment, he would want to be in the thick of it and he was I suspect the only surveying officer who was qualified to take up such an important post in war.

His loss means a lot to us over here, for he was well known and liked in the Admiralty and we fully expected that he would one day be the first Australian Hydrographer ...

It is not necessary for me to tell you to teach David to be proud of the memory and work of his Father; I know you will do that and if he grows up to be like him he will make a grand man ...

My love to you,
J.A. Edgell

Jim pondered over *Perth*'s short life — just two years and nine months' service in the Royal Australian Navy. This included the Atlantic, evacuation of troops from Greece and Crete, the battles of Matapan, the Java Sea and the heroic finale in the Sunda Strait. She reflected on many things ... Bill. Killed. Widowed. David. Navy.

Prior to the sinking of *Perth*, Jim had a vivid nightmare in which she had seen the ship in flames. The sheer terror of it had prompted her to share her anguish and confide in a friend, but she went to great lengths to conceal her fears from David. She had also written to the Navy telling them of her premonition. In it, she had seen her beloved Bill — Executive Officer and second-in-command — destroyed in *Perth*'s historic battle.

The loss of Perth claimed the lives of 353 men, unable to survive in the waters of Sunda Strait. Some one hundred were 'rescued' and captured by Japanese ships, only to die in servitude on the Burma–Thailand railway and other Japanese projects. Some died in ironic circumstances when US submarines sank one of the Japanese 'rescue' ships, *Rakuyo Maru*. Of Perth's crew of 682 men, only 229 survived to return home. The price had been high.

Captain Norman Harold Stephen (Knocker) White was one of the survivors. Over five decades later, he has total recall. Knocker (a standard Naval nickname) went to sea in 1936, aged sixteen. There were twelve in his term. HMAS *Canberra* was the RAN flagship at that time. He spent ten days aboard *Canberra* and was at sea the night war was declared against Germany — 3 September 1939. He joined *Perth* in January 1942 as a Sub-Lieutenant. Captain Hector (Hec) Waller, who had been his commander at the Royal Australian Naval College in 1936, was in charge. He had a distinguished war record, having commanded the 10th Destroyer Flotilla in the Mediterranean, and was highly regarded by both his Royal Navy contemporaries and his seniors. He was a dynamic officer, frighteningly efficient on the Bridge, harder on officers than on sailors. A man of capacity and character, respected and admired by all. It was a great pity that subsequent events did not allow Captain Waller to display all the leadership qualities he had demonstrated in the Mediterranean.

According to Knocker White, 'the polyglot group of ships that formed the striking force that fought in the battle of the Java Sea on 27 February 1942, the day prior to the night battle of the Sunda Strait, was almost totally destroyed. They were under the command of four different Navies and a Dutch Rear Admiral whose bravery was unquestioned, but he was very much a single ship man. Anyone who sailed in that striking force knew the utter improbability of the Dutch operating a disparate group of cruisers and destroyers against a highly efficient, well trained and formidable foe. A foe with first-class armament, outstanding optical equipment and torpedo and gunnery equipment, and, above all, trained to fight and cooperate with each other. We had absolutely no time to practise before we went into battle against them in the Battle of the Java Sea.'

Commander Bill Martin had joined *Perth* in Williamstown, Victoria, in February 1942 — just three weeks prior to its sinking. It was unusual for a hydrographer to be appointed Executive Officer of a six-inch cruiser, but Bill Martin had such a high regard for Hec Waller that he had written to him saying, 'I'm delighted that you've been appointed Commander of *Perth*. You're obviously going to need a good second-in-command — I'd like to be considered!'

Captain Waller was usually very formal and called the second-in-command 'Commander', but in the case of Bill Martin it was 'Bill'. Bill Martin was absolutely straight down the line, a man of considerable capacity, who fitted the role well. He was an excellent communicator with the sailors, who liked and respected him, a good seaman, gregarious, friendly, equally at ease with his Captain and officers. In the eyes of Knocker White, a Sub-Lieutenant who was in awe of Commanders and Executive Officers who are responsible for the running of the ship, Bill Martin was 'a delightful man to be serving with: friendly, extremely good to deal with, knowledgeable and very efficient'. He had a keen sense of humour and an apt turn of phrase. On one occasion he wrote to Knocker saying, 'I need an anti-gas officer. You have been lurked!'

Knocker recalls: '*Perth* was highly manoeuvrable with very good electrical equipment — a most efficient ship. During battles, until she was beginning to suffer damage during the Battle of Sunda Strait, there was not one mechanical or electrical breakdown. None of the guns failed to run out properly, there were no misfires, no gyro failures of any sort. Absolutely nothing went wrong. She was in top-class condition. Perhaps the only criticism is that *Perth* was in that area of the Java Sea at all, when it was far too late for even an efficient ship to be able to add very much to the strength of the Allied position, which was quite deplorable. It would have been better if the Naval Board had not decided to detach *Perth* from the ANZAC Force on the east coast of Australia [which later included the USS *Chicago*] and had instead sent her round to Western Australia and up to what became known as the ABDA [American, British, Dutch, Australian] area.'

However, the cold, hard facts remain. On 28 February 1942, *Perth* and USS *Houston* ran slap-bang into the main Japanese force landing on the west coast of Java: a convoy of some forty-odd transports at anchor in Bantam Bay, just before the entrance to Sunda Strait, supported by two eight-inch cruisers, three six-inch cruisers and three flotillas of destroyers. The forces against *Perth* and *Houston* were formidable. Just after 7 pm, Captain Waller had been advised there were no Japanese ships anywhere near the area. He had broadcast to the ship's company that he didn't expect to encounter enemy forces. As Knocker White recalls: 'We were in second degree of readiness at the time the first ship was sighted and, because there had been six Australian corvettes operating in the Sunda Strait area, Captain Waller said, "It is probably one of our corvettes". Then, recognising the silhouette of a Japanese destroyer, he gave the order to the Gunnery Officer to open fire.'

It was the sound of guns firing that awakened Knocker White. He had been rostered for the Middle Watch, midnight till 4 am. It was hot, humid and uncomfortable, and he was very tired. There was no air conditioning, and it was claustrophobic sleeping in the torpedo office. Knocker thought drowsily, 'We're probably only practising', but then quickly realised, 'No, we're in action', and made his way to his action station.

'*Perth* didn't sustain any damage at all in the Battle of the Java Sea, although straddled many, many times. We were not hit with a single shell, mainly thanks to the excellent ship handling by Captain Waller,' recalls Knocker. As it got close to midnight, *Perth* was taking quite a lot of shell hit and Commander Martin left the aft control, saying to Lieutenant John Thode, 'You wait here, Thode. I'm going down to deal with that fire'. He went to the Upper Deck to take charge of the fire and the repair parties who dealt with battle damage. It was the correct thing to do and Bill Martin did it.

It would have become fairly apparent to Bill by then that damage control was becoming critical, even though, at that time, *Perth* had not been hit by any torpedoes.

At 12.10 am, the first of four torpedoes hit *Perth* on the starboard side and killed everyone in the forward Engine Room. The first torpedo was only about 15 metres away from Knocker White's action station. There was an almighty bang, the lights went out, and everyone was flung onto the deck. Secondary lighting came on. There was an order from the Bridge from Captain Waller: 'Stand by — prepare to abandon ship'. A second torpedo hit. Knocker was the last one out of the Gunnery Control Centre. A third torpedo, then a fourth. Knocker stepped slowly and carefully over the port guardrail, which was almost awash, into the warm waters of Sunda Strait. He swam as fast as possible away from the ship, then turned on his back. 'I saw *Perth* sink from about 90 metres away, propellers turning, but the ship had almost stopped by then, bows down of course, listing heavily to port and moving very slowly forward. *Perth* did not turn over — she is still lying on her port side on the ocean floor. Divers, both Indonesian and Australian, and quite conceivably others, have dived on the "wreck" and possibly plundered her many times since 1 March 1942.' *Houston* was still afloat, and on fire.

Whilst swimming, Knocker heard a thin voice calling 'Mr White'. In the full moon, he saw the Gunner, John Ross, who said, 'I can't blow up my life jacket'. Knocker then realised that he was not wearing his own. He blew up the life jacket for Ross and steered him to an overloaded raft. As he put him on the raft, Knocker observed that one of the men was very badly wounded, crying out in pain, obviously dying, so he decided he wouldn't stay and swam on until he found a piece of wood. All night he clung to the wood and swam.

By dawn, Knocker was extremely weary, though still clutching the piece of wood. The morning wore on. There was no hope of being picked up. In his own words, 'I had two chances of survival, and Buckley's was one of them'.

As he despaired of survival, he was hauled aboard a boat which had floated off one of the merchant ships that had been sunk by either the Japanese or the Allies. There were some Australian sailors, a couple of officers and some *Perth* survivors on board. Polo Owen gave him a sip of water and cleaned the oil from his eyes, then everyone on that boat, at least twenty men, performed a mammoth task. Against the current, with five oars each side and two men to each oar, they rowed this monstrously heavy 27-foot British conventional steel lifeboat *back* towards Sangiang Island. The rowing was extraordinarily difficult and seemed to go on forever. Eventually they beached the boat on the southern side of the island, where they all collapsed and slept until nightfall. They then made their way through long, tall kunai grass and trees to deserted huts where they spent the night. There they remained for three to four days.

Lieutenant John Thode, who had abandoned ship earlier than Knocker, managed to land on Topper's Island, 6–8 kilometres to the north of Sangiang. There, he and other *Perth* survivors built a raft. The *Houston* survivors on Toppers wouldn't be in it, saying, 'We'll stay here — you Aussies are plumb crazy'. Then Thode and his team paddled the raft to Sangiang, downstream, and joined up with Polo Owen's team.

On about 4 March, they took off for the mainland of Java in the boat and, after a series of mishaps, arrived at Tjilatjap, on the south coast of Java, on 16 March, believing it was still in Dutch hands. It was not. The men were taken to a Japanese POW camp. Knocker White spent the next three and a half years as a captive of the Japanese.

Maxwell Keith Jagger (Dagsie) was another who came back. He joined *Perth* in October 1941 as an ordinary seaman, second class. He remembers the afternoon of 28 February, after the Battle of Java Sea, when Redlead — the ship's cat — had tried to desert. This was regarded by many sailors as bad luck, an omen. 'Get that bloody cat back', Commander Bill Martin had roared, and someone had raced down and done so. Always friendly, Bill Martin would be up in the aft control tower and Max and he would often exchange a wave.

'He was a wonderful seaman. We were a crack ship and Captain Hec Waller was the greatest skipper the RAN ever produced,' says Max. He knows the time he hit the water — his watch stopped at 12.05 am. It is among his possessions to this day, as a reminder of that fateful night and the following years.

Max was a powerful swimmer and, unlike Knocker White, he was wearing his life jacket. He swam for fourteen hours, picking up different people and getting them on to something that was floating, before arriving at Sangiang at two-thirty in the afternoon. Twelve of them spent thirty-eight days in an open boat, island-hopping around Sunda Strait and the islands on the south-east coast of Sumatra.

On 7 April 1942, they were taken as prisoners of war. They spent ninety-nine days in the local gaol, Telok Betong, and, on the ninety-eighth day, at 3 am, they were placed in chains and leg irons, loaded in a truck, and ultimately transferred to the slums of Palembang — 'a shocking place', Max recalls. 'Palembang was the worst-fed camp of the whole Japanese-operated territory.' Strong men, who were originally 90 kilogams, weighed in later at hospital in Singapore around 45 kilograms. These same men were described as 'fit for heavy duty'. This camp provided the labour throughout the entire war. They were responsible for all the dock work and the loading and unloading of every ship. Senior officers were taken away in September 1942 and sent up to Java. In January and February 1945, a group of 'light duty men', those who had been ill with dysentery or had lost a leg or had bad tropical ulcers, were 'sent to "The Cabbage Patch"', which is how they described the cemetery. A few hundred others went to Singapore. There was a very high death rate. The last figures at capitulation — and there were many more deaths afterwards — showed that the camp strength was down to about seven hundred, a far cry from the original number of four thousand. The death rate amongst the Dutch was over 60 per cent, the British sustained 44 per cent. The Australians only lost five out of a hundred and, of the twelve in the open boat trip off *Perth*, eleven came home. They survived on friendship and mateship.

'When you're living with the enemy, twenty-four hours a day, when you don't know if you'll be alive in the next five minutes, you search for support, become very close. You couldn't survive on your own — it'd be "The Cabbage Patch",' and, adds Max, 'this bond of mateship is very hard to describe. It's as strong as ever today. We see each other more as brothers than as friends. A loyal band of brothers with great interest in each other.'

Max is often asked if he can forgive and forget. He replies, 'There is no way in the world that you can ever forget — it's physically impossible, it's indelible. Forgive? There are no bygones. No one can forget or really forgive the atrocities, the bayonets, the beheadings, the executions, the shots, the riding crops, the beltings for nothing, the petrol and burnings alive of fellow men.'

The lessons of war endure. They serve as powerful reminders. Although Bill Martin had not returned, at least he had not suffered in POW camps and been stretched to the limits of human endurance. With a shudder at the recollection of what might have happened to Bill, Jim wondered, yet again, how she would fare when her only child — the apple of her eye — would depart for Flinders' Naval Base in just a few months time, at the tender age of thirteen. David Martin had a shining example to follow — he never wanted to be a red Indian or a train driver. The Navy was his dream. His father's death at sea, far from diverting him from that goal, instead inspired him.

CHAPTER THREE

THE CALL OF THE SEA

His officer-like qualities are well developed

Tuesday, 28 January 1947 finally dawned. It was hot; over 100 degrees on the Fahrenheit scale. Twenty-four thirteen-year-old boys, all from very different backgrounds, arrived in Melbourne to join the Royal Australian Navy.

Despite the heat some still had their overcoats draped over their arms, having come from as far away as Western Australia, no doubt instructed that Melbourne is always cold. Not during this heatwave!

They assembled at the Navy Office, Victoria Barracks, just off St Kilda Road, early that same afternoon. The *Geddes Act* of 1920/21 had cut the Services right back and had reduced the intake of cadets until the end of the war. This was the first big entry since then — almost the same number as in 1917 when Bill Martin entered the Royal Australian Naval College. David Martin was the 656th Cadet Midshipman to join and was among six of the twenty-four boys selected who were from Naval backgrounds. Late in 1946, 600 thirteen-year-old candidates had sat for the entrance examination and gone before a Naval Selection Committee seeking only two dozen boys who 'possessed the potential qualities of leadership, intelligence, initiative and responsibility'. As it turned out, the intake of 1947 was one of exceptional talent.

There was excitement in the air, lots of boys' talk on the bus, comparing which State was the best, how hard the entry examination had been, had the standard been met? Their powers of observation had been tested. Questions were hurled at them: 'How many steps did you ascend when coming to this office?'; 'How many carriages were there on the train coming down?'; 'How many lions on the Coat of Arms?'; 'If you saw a coin marked 54BC would it be a fake?'. George Halley (who became a great friend of David), when asked during the test for colour blindness, 'Is that colour green or blue?' replied, 'Neither — it's turquoise!'

The young Cadet Midshipmen arrived at Flinders Naval Depot, HMAS *Cerberus*, on Westernport Bay — the home of the Royal Australian Naval College from 1931 to 1957. Newly appointed Cadet Captains introduced the newcomers to college life, rules and regulations. They were issued with most of their kit the next day. The cadets glimpsed their cap badges with great pride. During the war and immediately afterwards, they used tin ones — the genuine articles were gold wire, which David knew since he had his father's. He whispered to George, 'You should see the real ones'.

David Martin loved everything about the place and wrote enthusiastically to his mother three days later, describing the round-the-clock activity of the cadets' day.

Following a hot splash from filled wash basins and a cold shower both summer and winter, the cadets sometimes went on a 'smart double' of about a kilometre to warm up before breakfast. At other times they read semaphores or carried out parade training.

After breakfast came sundry chores of boot cleaning and sweeping, then signals, then eight full hours of studies followed by two hours of sport in the late afternoon before an hour of study. By 9 pm they were out like lights! The cadets all thought it was wonderful. They were always doing something and the seasons were well marked with football and cricket.

The cadets often went on camping and boat picnics to Phillip Island or Mornington, and these were real survival exercises — quite an ordeal for the junior cadets. They were expected to participate in cross-country races of almost 10 kilometres.

Almost all the boys in the 1947 entry had fathers who had served in World War I or II, four of whom had paid the supreme sacrifice in

> Dear Mum,   31-1-47
>
> Just a short note to say that I am very well. I love it here: the meals are pretty good and everything is really top hole. We get up at 0700, fold back blankets, have showers and brush teeth. Get dressed and then have squad drill !!! Then we have breakfast. Then divisions on the quarter deck. Then we get yelled at in the gym for a solid hour then have bun + milk. Then have squad drill, then lunch, then squad drill then stand easy then squad drill then cricket, then swimming.
>
> All Air Mail Letters you send me cost 4ᵈ only
> " Ordinary "   "   "   "   1ᵖ   "
>
> So theres some good news for you. The other cadets return tonight, so we're waiting with quaking hearts. Thats all for now
>
> Love from David (C.M)

World War II. John Waller, Captain 'Hec' Waller's son, had, like David, lost his father in the sinking of *Perth*. The common background for this group of boys who had been brought up during the war ensured that they had an inbuilt sense of patriotism. Most of them had been Boy Scouts. Many of their mothers had wanted a son in the Navy. Today there are heroes on the football field, but back then the heroes were flying Spitfires or captaining destroyers.

The mission statement was simple; there were no hang-ups or problems. The Cadet Midshipmen were nurtured on the concepts of service, loyalty and team spirit. They were answering the call to adventure; in time they would travel, they would go to sea.

David's mid-year report from the Director of Studies stated that his performance was 'very satisfactory', and from the Commander, 'making satisfactory progress'. The annual report noted, 'It is felt that he will do better if he exercises greater concentration in the classroom'. The reports of 1948 commented, 'Satisfactory but too timid in effort. He must develop more determination. He is not sufficiently energetic.' However, by December 1949, the Director of Studies' report stated, 'He has continued to work conscientiously, and his results are very creditable'. The House Officer's report declared him 'A good Cadet. Has shown marked improvement during the year, and, if he maintains this, will make a good Cadet-Captain. Keen, conscientious, well mannered and loyal.' And from the Commodore Superintendent of Training, 'He has improved more than any Cadet in his year'. The final annual report, October 1950, confirmed his results. 'Position in Studies — 6 out of 20. Number of hours instruction lost through sickness — Nil.'

His Commander's report stated, 'His officer-like qualities are well developed', and the Commodore Superintendent of Training agreed: 'Not only has the young officer obtained very good results both in his studies and other activities, but has exerted an excellent influence at the College'.

In their last year at Naval College, Mr Simpson, Director of Studies, asked all the boys to select a 'decent book' of their choice, read it well and then discuss it in class. David decided it was more important for him to study for his history examination the next period, so he concealed his notes inside the book. Mr Simpson caught him and exclaimed, 'I have been a teacher for forty years and have often seen a novel inside a history book, but this is the first time I've ever found a history book inside a novel'. He passed!

When on leave from the College, David attended — and thoroughly enjoyed — many parties with old school friends from Scots College. Whilst at the Royal Australian Naval College, there was a dance at the end of each term. The cadets could invite their own partners or take 'pot luck' with the girls from Toorak Ladies College at Frankston. David and George had great fun at these dances, even though they ended as early as 11.30 pm. 'We used to take the night air with our partners', George remembers.

Even in his teens, David Martin was a natural leader. He was very keen on sport, a great tryer, and a very fast runner. On entry to the College, he was only 1.5 metres tall, though he eventually grew to 1.79 metres. He was Captain of the First Fifteen rugby team. He was plucky and could put on the gloves and hold his own in the boxing ring.

David became a Watch Cadet Captain in his final year. The watches were virtually school houses, and there were three — the Forecastle, the Quarterdeck and the Topmen. The victorious watch had a special victory dinner for each major competition on the sporting field. Thanks to David's leadership, the Topmen enjoyed many a celebratory dinner. He rallied all the cadets; they responded warmly and admired him as a 'fine fellow'.

The Passing Out Ceremony took place on 27 October 1950. Twenty Cadet Midshipmen graduated — the largest number since 1920. David graduated as a Senior Cadet Captain. Prime Minister Robert Menzies, who attended the ceremony, remarked, 'There is no such thing as a dumb politician', and proceeded to speak to them for twenty-five minutes! He concluded by urging them to 'render real service to the community'.

They had completed their first objective. The Royal Australian Naval College had turned out a product. These seventeen-year-olds were learning to command men and exercise leadership. Thanks to the Navy, in peace or war they would assume responsibility, exercise authority and demonstrate accountability. It had been a great apprenticeship. There had been fun, variety and challenge. Now it was over to the boys themselves. Life was opening up — they were now part of the show and everyone liked being in the act.

If only the Flinders Year Cadets of 1947 could see how conditions have improved since then. Cadet Midshipmen now have single cabins instead of six to a cabin, and men and women share the same accommodation building. There is no longer the same strict discipline and punishments. Midshipmen under training now receive well over $200 a week, not 1/6d a week for the first year. As 3d was deducted from their pay to go towards the Food for Britain Fund, there was very little left to spend or save. They not only assisted the fund financially, but responded to the Commander's invitation to visit his residence on Sunday afternoons to assist with packing the food parcels.

Early in December 1950, David Martin, George Halley and the other cadets sailed to England in *Strathhaird,* delighting in all the fun that this passenger liner had to offer. In those days, farewelling P&O and Orient liners was a great social event. There were cabin parties, streamers, tears, laughter and many fond goodbyes. Shipboard life was all they expected it to be. Dressing for dinner was good fun and the menus were all that healthy young men could handle — most of them had every course. They also participated in deck sports, the favourite being deck tennis. All of this activity worked up an appetite for the next meal!

Once the cadets arrived in England in 1951, they spent eight months working together as 'hands' aboard the training cruiser, HMS *Devonshire,* from the West Indies to Scandinavia. The objective was to ensure that the young gentlemen knew how men lived in a ship. They performed all the skivvy duties and spent their time either working hard or trying hard to get out of work! They also did a great deal of classroom work, studying seamanship, engineering and navigation. Manning and running the ship's boats to and from the shore or jetty when the ship was at anchor was great fun.

The cadets gained much practical experience and established lifelong friendships with other cadets from all over the British Commonwealth, as well as Burma and Ireland. Looking back over forty-five years, George Halley remembers the fun times more than some of the grim moments. 'The travel was rewarding, visiting the Spainish main and Norway where the sea traditions have been manifest over the centuries. We also learnt a great deal about self-discipline and leadership. We were very glad when it was all over and we were promoted to Midshipmen. We had been Cadet Midshipmen for nearly five years.'

On his return to Australia, Midshipman David Martin, now eighteen, saw active service in the Korean War in HMAS *Sydney*. An operational aircraft carrier, she held the record for the most launchings and landings of combat aircraft in the Korean War. His Commanding Officer was David (Darbo) Harries, a man of few words who had been in the same entry into the Royal Australian Naval College as David's father. After David had been in the ship several months, Admiral Harries inquired if he was W.H. Martin's son. Young Midshipman Martin thought, 'At last! The great man will talk about my father.' 'Yes, sir', he replied. The taciturn Captain uttered, 'I knew him'.

After a period in *Sydney*, from September 1951 to December 1952, David and George Halley were together once more when they were posted to HMAS *Murchison*, a River Class frigate. Promotions were steady for David. He became Acting Sub-Lieutenant in January 1953, Sub-Lieutenant in October 1954, and in July 1955 he was promoted to Lieutenant.

Meanwhile, in March 1953, it was back to England again, this time on board *Strathmore*, for more fun, followed by two memorable terms at the famous Royal Naval College at Greenwich. It was in *Strathmore* that David and George participated in a fancy dress party. George was King Richard the Lionheart and David and Mike Varley were the horse. Right in front of the judges, David let forth a superb whinnying noise and Mike, who was the horse's rear, emptied a large bag of sawdust on the dance floor. Needless to say, they won first prize.

The year 1953 was a magnificent time to be in London — it was Coronation year, which marked the birth of the new Elizabethan age. The whole atmosphere leading up to the Coronation moved and motivated David. He enjoyed everything that England offered. In addition to the fun of the London 'season', he and George stayed with friends in the country at Hereford, where they attended country dances which began about 10 pm and lasted till dawn, a band from London belting out popular tunes. It was white tie and champagne all the way and 'we lapped it up quite well', recalls George.

David wrote to his mother about the Coronation of Queen Elizabeth II, the second Coronation he had experienced in his life.

... George and I were so placed that by stretching and bending our necks we could see about 150 yards up the Mall, by looking a bit to our right we could see right up Constitution Hill as far as Hyde Park Corner, and in front of us was the Palace. Couldn't have been better ...

We waited there till 1027, when the Queen's Procession started — they had filed past us and were halted in the Mall, waiting for the coach ... Then they moved off and the Royal Coach came into view. The scene was beyond description — despite the weather it was breathtaking. Slowly the glorious greys pulled the coach past us — we could see inside the coach very well, and there they were; she, strained but gracious and charming, looking very small and delightfully attractive; he, composed and obviously reassuring to her, smiling and waving with her. I had expected a thrill, but this was something else — I felt intensely proud and had that feeling where one doesn't know whether to smile or weep. The tears in my eyes weren't from sneezing anyhow ... It was a sight I shall never forget.

Being in England afforded David the chance to visit the Continent, including a memorable fortnight at a little ski resort, Berwang, in the Austrian Tyrol. The Austrians, who celebrate Christmas as a religious festival, reserve all their frivolity for the New Year. David and three other Sub-Lieutenants found themselves at a small village restaurant at about 7 am on New Year's Day, very tired, very hungry and with very little German at their disposal. David thereupon made an incredible noise — a cross between a pig and a chook — and, somehow, the Austrian hausfrau understood that they'd like ham and eggs for breakfast!

Back in England, David diligently applied himself to his Service studies. After completing technical courses in Portsmouth, he returned to Australia at the end of 1954 in the Orient liner *Orcades*. Just like his father and mother before him, he had a wonderful shipboard romance which led to a marriage partnership lasting thirty-three years.

CHAPTER FOUR

A SHIPBOARD ROMANCE

This is it, I reckon

They were both travelling with their mothers. The Martins, Jim and David, were returning to Australia from England. The Millears, mother Sylvia and daughter Suzanne, embarked at Naples and were heading home to Victoria, where their lively family of four men — husband and three sons — awaited.

He was twenty-one. She was eighteen. Mutual friends had alerted both parties to look out for the other. They met on day one, 15 November 1954. With a smile, Susie said, 'Oh, I know who you are, you're David Watson'. With a smile he replied, 'No, no, I'm David Martin'. The die was cast. They chatted for a couple of hours, then David went to his cabin. Jim took one look at him and observed, 'You're in love'. David could only agree.

His diary entry for that day reports, 'Sue Millear got on today and I got me a stomach full of butterflies'. By day two she was 'a grand girl'. She didn't rate a mention on day three, but by day four, 'The night was made for us — stars, moon, peace and quiet and the port for'ard glassed-in corner to ourselves'. He wrote that he was 'more than interested'. On Saturday, 20 November, he wrote, 'Feeling a bit sick, sore shoulders, tired. Sue fixed them all for me. Went to the Galle Face Hotel — good meal, good band, good dancing, good Sue.' The next day's entry reports 'she's tops' and on 28 November he 'turned in profoundly happy. This is it, I reckon'.

Susie's diary was equally complimentary. On day one she wrote, 'Met David Martin — he's a pet'. On Saturday, 20 November, she too 'got very burnt — quite puce', but she was well over her sunburn six days later when she confessed, 'This trip is just too blissful for words ... I do love David, he really is a poppet'.

So, just eleven days after they met, the scene was set. They spent three exhilarating weeks on board, revelling in each other's company, dancing until dawn, gazing into each other's eyes as the music played their favourite tune, 'It Was Just One of Those Things'. On the way home, there were visits to Port Said and Colombo, where they were fascinated by the magic of the gilly gilly man, as well as brief stops in Perth and Adelaide to catch up with family.

Once back in Australia, there were letters to and fro, and Susie came to Sydney a few times to see David before she began nursing at the Alfred Hospital in Melbourne in 1955, earning £3.15 a week.

Suzanne Millear attended Clyde School from 1945 to 1953, and was raised near Willaura in the western district of Victoria. Her father, Spencer Millear, was a grazier whose family had been graziers in Australia for three generations. The Millears also own a large sheep stud near Warren in New South Wales and have been breeding merinos for over one hundred years.

David, on the other hand, like all young Naval officers at the time, had no assets. Even Edna Little, his doting aunt, thought he was 'very lucky to get her — no doubt her parents would have preferred a grazier to a sailor'. And all of Susie's uncles kept telling her, 'Don't do it — you don't know what you are letting yourself in for'.

In 1955, David sailed for England again, this time in the aircraft carrier HMAS *Vengeance*, returning a year later in a new aircraft carrier HMAS *Melbourne*. A case of taking over the old and bringing back the new. The Royal Australian Navy had borrowed *Vengeance* from the Royal Navy whilst *Melbourne* was modernised with the addition of an angled flightdeck, landing mirror and steam catapult.

David took up a new position as Training Officer at HMAS *Torrens*, a recruitment and training establishment in Adelaide, in May 1956. He would occasionally visit Susie at the property on weekends when she was off duty. Arriving by train, he would get in at 3.30 am and she would drive in the pitch black to collect him. On Sunday nights he would take a train back at 11.30 pm. It was on the train from Ararat to Melbourne at 5 am on 15 May that David proposed, both of them huddled under a rug. Probably because she was so cold, Susie replied, 'I don't know', which David thought was ungracious, so she amended it to 'Yes, alright', which he didn't think was very romantic of her either! However, he still returned to Ararat for many other weekends and, quite early in the piece, asked her father's permission to marry. Grinning broadly, he came out of the study declaring, 'Everything's alright!'. There were kisses, tears, hugs and lots of champagne.

A six-month engagement followed. Everyone in the family got on beautifully. Jim and Susie had liked each other the moment they first met. To Susie, Jim was 'a lovely, gentle, quiet creature' and, although a serious person, possessed an excellent sense of humour. David was their common love. Susie's mother, Sylvia, was delighted with the match, all the brothers loved him and, after a hesitant start, father and prospective son-in-law developed a great respect for each other.

During this time, Susie gave up nursing and went home to the family property, 125 kilometres west of Melbourne. There was a wedding to plan. 'A lovely wedding', 'A small wedding, Dad'. They began to make lists. Her father agreed in principle to keeping it small, but repeatedly said, 'You've got to have him because he really has been very good to us' and, 'You couldn't leave him out — he's a good bloke', so they ended up having everyone they'd ever heard of and lots of people they'd never heard of! 'The little wooden turn-of-the century church seated only eighty people, so the others didn't get in or they waited outside', Susie recalls.

The day of the wedding — 5 January 1957 — arrived. It was midsummer and stifling. There was a dust storm and the only Millear daughter arrived at All Saints Church, Willaura, with mosquitoes and grasshoppers all through her veil! It didn't matter to David, though, who described Susie as 'breathtaking'. His best man was George

Halley. When George rose to speak at the reception he could hear David's words 'keep it short' ringing in his ears, so he delivered what must be one of the shortest speeches of all time — 'As King Solomon said to the Queen of Sheba, "Madam, I've not come here to talk"' — and sat down! The reception was held in the grounds of the Millear's home — fortunately, under a marquee!

Sylvia Millear thought she'd provide a luncheon for the newlyweds the next day, so she booked them in close by at The Shakespeare Hotel in Great Western, just the other side of Ararat, for their first night. The 'lovely surprise' turned out to be a big mistake. It was a nasty, rather than charming, little country hotel. As he led them down a long passage where all the floor boards were up, the hotel keeper remarked, 'Not very smart, but I guess youse only wanna see the bed!'. Then it was through a concrete courtyard into the bedroom, where there was not one but four wrought iron beds, all with sagging mattresses. As he left, their host called over his shoulder, 'If youse wanna go, then it's through the chookyard!'.

The next day, after lunch, it was off to catch a plane to Brisbane, where they stayed overnight at Lennon's, then on to Surfers Paradise, where the service was more gracious and the facilities far better than at the Shakespeare!

David had wanted to go up the Hawkesbury on a boat for the honeymoon, but Spencer Millear said, 'You're going to New Zealand and I'm paying for it'. David responded, 'I'm sorry, Boss, but we're not going to New Zealand, we don't want your money and we're going where we want to go'. Many years later, Susie's father said to David: 'With the money I was prepared to spend on your honeymoon, I bought some steers. I sold them last week and here's the profit.' This time David accepted graciously.

The honeymoon over, David and Susie went to Adelaide to commence married life in a horse trainer's house. It smelled of dogs and horses, but they were too happy to mind very much. They painted the bathroom vivid blue for brightness and freshness, and did all they could to make everything as clean as possible.

As soon as they were settled in their new home, they were off in the P&O liner *Himalaya* to England, where David did the Long

Gunnery Course at HMS *Excellent*. This was to have been for two and a half years, but the course was split into two parts and David served a two year exchange with the Royal Navy. Consequently, they were away from Australia for four and a half years, during which time they had two daughters. Sandra (Sandy) was born in Portsmouth on 14 April 1958. George Halley was godfather. Joanna (Anna) was born on 3 September 1959 whilst they were living in Malta. David was then on exchange, as Gunnery Officer, in HMS *Battleaxe*, a Weapon Class destroyer. It was a year's posting in the Mediterranean, during which *Battleaxe* patrolled Cypriot waters as it was the time of the Cyprus Emergency.

David had been home on each occasion when they discovered they were to be parents, and was there for the birth of Sandy, their eldest. When Susie was pregnant with Anna, however, he was away for six months and returned to a one-month-old child. Sometimes seamen did not see their babies for several months.

On another occasion, whilst their husbands were at sea, several of the Naval wives decided to go together from the United Kingdom to Malta. David and Susie had many wonderful reunions and once went to Rome for four days. As usual, the return to day-to-day life meant it was back to putting out the garbage and being responsible for the upbringing of children who, although stimulating, were hardly able to substitute for a husband's presence. The ceaseless absences and accompanying loneliness led, in some cases, to marriage breakdowns, but Susie and David's trust in each other grew and strengthened. To their friends they were 'a good blend' and 'just right for each other'. David openly admired the demanding job which Susie, and other wives who shared their husbands' career pressures, undertook. In fact, he thought they all deserved medals, since they were the ones left on shore to deal with broken drains, bank managers, lost dogs, flat tyres, bounced cheques and sundry other difficulties while their husbands were away at sea. 'She has to be a special sort of person', he often remarked. 'You inevitably appreciate and respect a person like that. That is the reason Navy marriages are "pretty sound" once they survive the initial traumas.' He realised that being the heart of the family, as well as mother, father, cook and cleaner, requires great strength, lots of character and resourcefulness. He also knew that those same characteristics help to keep a good marriage alive.

With David's persistent absences, often for six months at a time, pen to paper was their main means of communication. Not all sailors are good correspondents — it is just more work at the end of a long and tiring day — but David was a dedicated letter writer. It was history repeating itself: as a child, he had often seen Jim doing exactly the same thing.

Missing his children, David kept in touch by inventing the most marvellous stories — from anything about the sea and adventure to goldfish and animals — which he put on tape as well as in letters. The children would gather round their tape machine and listen, enraptured, laughing at every situation, wide-eyed with wonder at some of the stories he told of a Japanese girl called Suki-Yuki and her fish. Today those lovely stories, still beautifully told, are passed on to his grandchildren as bedtime stories. At other times, when he heard from Susie that the children had been naughty, he would rebuke them on tape, only to find that by the time it arrived, they had been good for three weeks! Realising the timing was wrong and that he was confusing them, he left the disciplining to Susie.

Every marriage brings a few surprises — in this case it was the discovery that David was a sleepwalker. Each Naval rank, too, brings its own responsibilities and worries, and occasionally, when overtired or overstressed, David would talk and laugh in his sleep, his vivid imagination working overtime. It was never frightening, although he did get up to some strange things and found himself in the most peculiar situations. On one occasion, whilst staying with his mother-in-law, he ripped up all the handtowels in the bathroom. He was distraught once he realised. He needn't have worried — Sylvia Millear had a good sense of humour! Another time at sea, he woke up a great distance from his cabin. Fortunately he didn't wander on to the quarterdeck and walk right off, straight into the ocean. Nobody would have known why and may have presumed other motives.

In the English summer of 1960, the Martins moved to married

quarters outside Portsmouth. They remained there for several months whilst David completed the Long Gunnery Course. The houses were unattractive, but they had English as well as Australian Naval families living in them and they all liked each other and got along very well.

At the beginning of 1961, when they returned to Australia, Susie and David purchased their first home, a little cottage in Bellevue Hill in Sydney's Eastern Suburbs, not very far from Double Bay where David had lived as a child. Between them they paid £8000. The house had two mortgages on it: Spencer Millear helped and collectively they paid for it. Susie and David were both pleased to be back in Australia and delighted to know that, once again, another little Martin was on the way. 'A mid-summer's baby', they thought. 'What a great Australian Christmas gift!' The best laid plans ...

William was born on mid-winter's day, 21 Dec 1963. In England. He was truly an international baby — conceived in Hong Kong, Australian-made but born in England! Spencer Millear had sent Susie to Hong Kong for a holiday when David was away at sea for several months in the Australian Daring Class destroyer, HMAS *Voyager*, as Gunnery Officer. When David arrived in Hong Kong, Susie was there to meet him and they stayed at the 'Y'. Years later William joined the Navy and, arriving in Hong Kong, bought a postcard of the 'Y', which he sent to his mother with just two words on it: 'Déja Vu'. Still more years later, in 1995, William and Susie went to Hong Kong together, and he insisted 'We have to stay at the "Y"'! They did. Now called 'The Salisbury', upstairs it has remained exactly the same old 'Y'.

David's mother, Jim, had come to England in 1963 for the birth of her third grandchild. She arrived on 20 December and Susie came to meet her at the airport after dropping the girls off at school. David, too, met her, going straight to the airport from Australia House. They all drove back home in their little green Austin. When they had settled Jim in, Susie announced she was in labour, so it was off to hospital for the birth of Martin number three.

In 1963 and 1964, David was the Gunnery Officer on the staff at the Australian High Commission in London. By good fortune, he had been posted there from *Voyager* just a few months prior to its fatal collision with the aircraft carrier *Melbourne*. This tragedy occurred off

Jervis Bay on the night of 10 February 1964. Eighty-two officers and sailors on board the destroyer lost their lives. It was one of the darkest moments in Australia's Naval history and the RAN's worst catastrophe during peace time.

In 1967, Commander David Martin was called to give evidence at the sensational second inquiry into the disaster, held some time after the initial investigation. As Tony Stephens reported in the *Sydney Morning Herald*, 'the first inquiry blamed *Voyager* but not Captain Duncan Stephens. It criticised three officers of *Melbourne* ... Martin gave evidence to the second inquiry, supporting the thrust, though not the detail, of claims by Lieutenant-Commander Peter Cabban that Captain Stephens had a health problem (an ulcer), which was made worse by alcohol. This inquiry found that *Voyager* was at fault and, although Stephens was not a drunkard, his health should have made him unfit for command. Captain R.J. Robertson, who had lost command of *Melbourne* because of the collision, was exonerated.'

'I was very frightened at that inquiry', David admitted later. 'Relatively senior people had advised me not to rock the boat.'

Senior Naval Staff had warned David that he could jeopardise his future career by testifying — when going for Flag Rank it is usual to look after your existence! However, David always spoke his mind and had the courage to say what he believed in. Nor would he consciously have varied from the truth, even if that evidence proved to be damaging to himself. This was a great test of character for him, and led subsequently to a loss of confidence in Naval authority. In the process, a few enemies were made. Several people folded under pressure, there was conjecture, blame and a variety of views were held about the cause of the collision — 'a possible gyro compass failure', 'confusion in interpreting the signal', 'it was pitch black', 'vision was poor', 'nobody really knows' and 'nobody wants to talk' — but the fact remains that this incident is one of the saddest chapters in Australia's Naval history and — three decades later on — it remains an unparalleled disaster and questions still continue to be raised. In September 1995, compensation was finally granted to six of the survivors — thirty-one years after the tragedy which saw *Voyager* sliced in half.

The London appointment was for three years and Susie and David rented a house at Barnes. They also let their Sydney home. When David began a course at The Royal Naval College, Greenwich, they moved to a very nice part of an old house in Blackheath.

The Martins returned to Australia in 1966, longing to see and enjoy their little house in Bellevue Hill. They were aghast at what they saw. During their time away there had been four sets of tenants. The 'sweet little cottage' was putrid. The baking tray — still in the oven — and griller were full of furry, mouldy fat; the dining table was marked indelibly by scribbling; rancid water was still in vases; and when the curtains were pulled apart, they discovered that broken eggs, still in their shells, had been holding them together. When they called the estate agent demanding an explanation, they were further dismayed to hear, 'Don't know what you're worried about — they all paid the rent'.

Things are better now, but in those days there was no redress from the Navy for damaged property when personnel were posted elsewhere for long periods. David and Susie learned a valuable lesson for life: 'Never let a property furnished'.

As Christmas 1966 drew near, the bi-annual listings of promotions came out. Lieutenant Commander David Martin was promoted to Commander. Whereas promotion to Lieutenant Commander was then automatic, promotion to Commander was based entirely on merit. It was a big jump. He was thrilled and greatly excited. Commander! He had now reached equal status to his father.

Though promoted, one is placed on what is called 'the pregnant list' and it is not until six months later when the next list comes out that it is possible to 'put up your stripes'. So, in January 1967, Lieutenant Commander Martin went to sea as Executive Officer in HMAS *Vampire*, a sister ship of *Voyager*, for her tour of duty in South-East Asia.

He was soon required to take up the position of Commander of the Royal Australian Naval College, HMAS *Creswell*, so had to leave *Vampire* after six months. He did not like leaving so soon, because he felt he'd had insufficient time to get to know the officers of this destroyer, with number 11 on the side, which today is in the Australian National Maritime Museum at Darling Harbour.

Wearing his Commander stripes, he went down to the Naval College at Jervis Bay as second-in-charge on 15 July 1967. The following eighteen months, from mid-1967 to the end of 1968, were the best of times. Sandy and Anna went to a little public school in the grounds of the college and Will to nursery school. Susie learned to play golf and tennis, skills which have stood her in good stead ever since. It was a peaceful, enjoyable and very happy time.

Back in Sydney, in late 1968, they 'gave away' their house in Bellevue Hill for $27 000. Twenty years later, when they tried to buy back into Rivers Street, houses were bringing in the vicinity of $600 000. They then bought a house in Hopetoun Avenue, Vaucluse, with a flat downstairs for Jim, where they remained until mid-1972. It was their longest period staying in one place. The girls attended school at Kambala, Rose Bay, and William went to Vaucluse Public School until the next move, four years later.

David Martin had now spent over twenty years in the Royal Australian Navy, and during that period his career had progressed pleasingly. His next appointment, in 1969, for a duration of eighteen months, was to HMAS *Queenborough* as her Commanding Officer. This promotion elated him. He was also very much aware of the responsibility he held to the ship's company as well as to the ship. This command prepared him for his next posting: Fleet Operations Officer. This challenging role involved planning, preparing, organising and implementing the Fleet Programs, including visits by ships to Australian and overseas ports. As the Fleet Operations Officer accompanied the Fleet Commander (now known as the Martime Commander), these were tiring, taxing and exhilarating times. David served as Fleet Operations Officer from mid-1970 until July 1972. The family then went to Canberra, where he attended the Joint Services Staff College (JSSC), referred to as 'The Sewerage Farm' because of its proximity to that place! As the word 'joint' suggests, the College is tri-service, including not only the Navy but the Airforce and Army as well.

At the completion of that course, in December 1972, Commander David Martin was promoted to the rank of Captain and was posted to the Navy Office in Canberra.

CHAPTER FIVE

SHIP SPIRIT

There'll never be another one like that

Dusty, Tiger, Harry the Horse, Mother Superior, Have-a-Chat, Possum, Fanny, Smouge, Weary, Cow and The Mobile Maggot were just a few of the names bestowed by the lower deck — sailors' views of the officers they dealt with. Everyone knew it, no one seemed to mind. All Martins in the Navy were called 'Pincher', originally an old British term. David always referred to James Fahey as 'Curly Wee', whilst 'DJ' was James' favourite appellation. It was straight to the point, direct and friendly like its owner.

They met in *Vengeance* in 1955. James was a newly commissioned engineer, a 'round rig' ex-sailor who found the transition from the lower deck to Wardroom (the officer's mess), a traumatic experience. This difficult task was made easier for him and for many others by David Martin, who always accepted people for what they were. To Curly, DJ was 'a true gentleman in life'. He was caring, fun-loving, a born leader with a great capacity for communicating with people of all ranks. He disliked pretension and was never rude to others; instead, he would simply avoid them if necessary, and would not allow anyone or anything to spoil his enjoyment of every minute of every day.

'I never met a person quite like him in my life', says James of his friend of forty years. 'David Martin would have achieved greatness without even trying, greatness was in him. He had a deep belief in God which was carried through in everything he did. This was quite a rarity amongst Naval people.'

James Fahey had intended to be a Jesuit priest, instead he joined the Navy. Most of the people he went to school with were killed in World War II, and by the end of the war there were only two left. Everyone in the Navy of that vintage respected — more, loved — the Queen, and had taken the oath of allegiance to her father before her.

In *Vengeance*, DJ had middle watch on the Bridge, Curly had middle watch in the Engine Room — known as the ''Orrid 'Ot Engine Room'. Sometimes, in the early hours of the morning, David would ring down to the Engine Room and say, 'Have you got the toasted steak sandwiches ready yet?'. The stokers, who were 'a bunch of villains' and could make do with just about anything in terms of equipment, would oblige with ham and eggs sandwiched between thick, toasted bread, wrapped in foil, to keep the appetite assuaged! The food at sea was often indifferent, but at least it was wholesome and sustaining. The early morning sandwiches were a luxury.

At other times the crew would play team games, which always helped communication, as well as tombola, generally known as bingo, and housie, and there was always time for a few harmless dirty yarns!

Each ship is a little city of its own. Unlike the Army and Airforce, those in the Navy produced their own fresh water from sea water — tonnes and tonnes per day — generated their own electricity, baked their own bread. This tightly knit village formed part of the larger Naval family. Friendships were made and continued for life. Even if separated for years, they would just pick up where they had left off. James Fahey says it was 'the greatest life on earth — a little like a circus in that there was a group of performers, a few clowns and some very clever people'.

A ship is a little like a court of law, too. On one occasion there was a punch-up among the stokers, and David spotted a sailor sporting a cut lip. Raising an eyebrow, he enquired, 'Who gave you that lot?'. 'Nobody gave it to me — I had to work very hard for it', came the reply. Because he enjoyed the quip, instead of letting the 'punishment fit the crime', he merely admonished the sailor.

David's approach to discipline was usually appreciated, rarely abused and often resulted in better behaviour. He believed that discipline in a family, and in a ship, must be adaptable. In the Navy, he regarded discipline as a classic example of organised commonsense, based on the need to create an environment in which each person is able to get on with the job while living in close harmony with other people. He believed that the rights of every individual are precious but should not be put before the needs of the ship's company as a whole. The Captain needs to create and be part of a team to which all of the crew is proud to belong, and which they want to protect. As the leader, the Captain must discover, isolate and eliminate factors which irritate or disrupt; he needs to uphold, develop and proclaim ideals, goals and standards which make sense and which are achievable. Qualities such as mutual respect, understanding, trust, honesty, loyalty, cleanliness, tolerance and fun are essential elements in that web of discipline, but they don't just happen without guidance and leadership. They don't just happen in a family or in a nation either.

'Average youngsters from average homes join the Navy — they are offered leadership, which gives them a sense of purpose, a sense of direction, a sense of belonging and a sense of satisfaction. This could be achieved throughout Australia, starting in families,' David once wrote. He gave trust to the ultimate degree. Both on land and at sea, David could quickly separate the dedicated from the dabblers.

The Navy demonstrates from day one that a strong family spirit — ship spirit — can withstand almost any pressure. Each ship's company is a family, and like every family it needs leadership. It is taught early in the Navy that the position held by 'The Old Man' doesn't mean privilege or status — it means obligation, responsibility and service.

David had a great commitment to the family and realised the need for everyone in society to pull together. He called it teamwork and acknowledged that 'excellence is a respectable goal … Competition is vital. Success is not a dirty word, particularly if success in high places is achieved honourably.'

He was often father and guide to thousands of young seamen who served under him in his years in the Navy. He made his home, whether in England, Malta or Cyprus, a home for many Naval officers of different nationalities who found themselves on shore, lonely and far from home.

Harold Adams was in the intake directly before David Martin. The Adams family owned a farm in central Victoria. Harold attended Melbourne Grammar School with the Millear boys, Susie Martin's brothers. Whilst the Millears were very happy on the land, Harold wasn't particularly attracted to farming. His family had a tradition of military service in both wars, and although none had ever served in the Navy, it had a very strong appeal to him, as it did for many of his school friends. As a small boy, he had read many stories of Naval successes during the war. So, although Harold had won a scholarship to the Senior School of Melbourne Grammar, he joined the Navy at Flinders Naval Depot in Januray 1946, aged thirteen. (Thirty-three years later, he returned there in command.)

After four years at the Royal Australian Navy College, Harold eventually went to sea in 1950 as a Midshipman, and in 1951 saw operational service in Korea. Although a year ahead of David, his early career path was virtually identical, including two terms at the Royal Naval College, Greenwich. Thereafter, their careers followed similar patterns of seagoing and shore postings and courses. They served together on the Naval staff at Australia House in London in 1963–64. They remained firm friends for life.

Harold Adams' regard for David Martin hasn't changed. He always admired his enthusiasm, his love of involvement, his outgoing personality and his ability as a 'people person'. 'There is no doubt he was an achiever, and a good crisis manager to boot — and always good company.'

~

'He was like a mosquito coil — he just drew people to him', says Leo Duffy, Commander David Martin's Petty Officer for two years in *Queenborough*, which had a complement of 250 officers and sailors. On this small, old, comfortable ship — a Q class anti-submarine frigate — they met for the first time and formed a friendship. Leo says unashamedly, 'I'd walk or crawl over broken glass for him'.

Queenborough was David's first command — he followed George Halley on 15 February 1969. George asked him to be the last to sign his visitors' book and David happily obliged, writing, 'Move over,

George. Thank you.' Leo was singled out to look after Captain Martin as his Steward. Right from the start, Leo knew where he stood with David. 'He always called a spade a spade. There were no in-betweens — either yes or no.' He immediately respected David and knew it was going to be 'terrific'.

Leo had joined the Navy at nineteen. Coming from a farm in Queensland, he applied and was rejected — his spelling let him down. However, determined to follow in his father's footsteps and convinced that the Navy was the place for him, he returned home and got the local teacher to help him. He then reapplied. This time he was accepted and went to what was then Flinders Naval Depot, HMAS *Cerberus*, a land base.

His father, Michael John Duffy, had been a Gunnery Officer and had attained the rank of Lieutenant Commander. As a child, Leo had been enthralled by what his father had to tell and show him. He would visit his father on ships and dream of the time he too could go to sea.

Leo's duties as Steward were varied, including looking after uniforms and shoes, ensuring they were spotless, doing the ironing in the cabin or quarters and the laundry if necessary. David was very particular in his dress. Together they made sure that his outfits were perfect. Though David was fastidious about some things, he was patient about others. 'Unless you really stuffed up, he rarely lost his cool, preferring instead to reason and reassure', Leo recalls with a wry smile. 'We must have better timing' or 'Let's refine this', he'd say to Leo. It was always 'we' rather than 'you', because he realised that nothing came on a silver platter — one had to work at things and there were often extenuating circumstances.

David felt his role was to help solve problems rather than create them. Meals coming right up from the Galley below may not have been quite as hot as they could have been, but he never said 'That's your problem', instead it was 'our' problem. He'd listen and absorb, then say, 'Leo, let's try it this way'. He didn't bark before he'd bite and this suited everyone.

David loved his food but was neither a big eater nor a big drinker. He would always save one last special mouthful which included a little of everything. At official functions he would usually have only one gin and tonic. He was very fit, never overweight and although sometimes at sea he was sick, 'If he was crook or had the 'flu, even then he was good humoured'.

David also loved his coffee — not standard coffee, but 'black and two'. On the Bridge, which he couldn't leave, he kept his own special coffee mug and liked a fresh coffee at hourly intervals. Both Leo and the Yeoman (the Chief Petty Officer Signalman), who was also very close to David, knew exactly how and when he wanted things done and 'nine times out of ten it would come off'. Those on duty would rise early, sometimes as early as 4 am. 'The Bosun's mate would normally do the shakes [the wake-up shakes] if the request was before 6.30 am, otherwise the shrill Bosun's call shattered sleep!' Leo would then get up, have a quick wash and, depending on the water restrictions (which varied from thirty seconds to three minutes because the stokers had to make the water continuously), would bring David 'a cuppa' to greet the day.

'He became like a father to me — I looked up to and respected him. He just seemed to give you that assurance and self-esteem,' Leo recalls.

David was a stickler for punctuality, so Leo was always five minutes early. 'Sometimes the gear would be ready the day before and often there would be two of everything — just in case!' remembers Leo. It was worth it because David was always quick to appreciate the effort. 'Thank you, Leo. That was terrific,' he'd smile and nod approvingly. 'And what a handshake! Not a flimsy one, a steady one,' says Leo.

At sea David had photos of his family around him. They followed him wherever he sailed. Leo remembers the little Martins, as they were then, coming on board *Queenborough*. 'Always very polite,' he says, 'and they've never lost it.' Sometimes when the ship was coming in to Sydney after dark, David would say, 'Let's pick out our house', so Leo and the Yeoman would get a little torch and flash a signal to the house and the children would flick the light switch on and off in recognition.

When he was at the Boss's table dealing with disciplinary matters, David would first look for a way out for the offenders rather than inflict a punishment. 'I'll give you ten minutes to think up a really good excuse', he'd instruct, trying to give the offenders a chance to avoid a penalty. In the course of this procedure he heard some weird and wonderful tales — 'absolute beauties' — but he never seemed to lose his legendary sense of humour.

David personally checked the wine books every two weeks, which saved Leo doing the bookwork, to keep the officers in tow. When doing exercises with other ships, there was always a 'no drink' order for sailors, and officers were always 'dry' at sea. Normally there was no 'beer issue' the first night out because everyone was settling in and, having had enough before going to sea, they were in for a dry period. However, when in harbour, David had said to Leo, 'Help yourself to the fridge ... in moderation', and Leo never abused that trust.

Leo Duffy left the Navy in June 1986, after almost twenty-four years in the Service. He didn't like the thought of being posted to *Cerberus* in Victoria when his home had been finally built in New South Wales. He was looking for a more relaxed way of life. Also, at that time the Navy had introduced women to sea and he 'couldn't see it working'.

To Leo, David Martin was the Boss, the Captain, Pincher and family. 'Every time you'd see him it would lift you up a bit. He did something to you. There'll never be another one like that.'

CHAPTER SIX

From Torrens to Tresco

And wasn't it all beaut?

The 1970s were exhilarating years for David Martin, his service career going from strength to strength.

In 1973, he was the newly appointed Director of Naval Reserves and Cadets at the Navy Office in Canberra. He had about a million dollars at his disposal and was responsible for almost four thousand cadets throughout Australia. 'I've no immediate plans to reorganise the reserves of the cadets, I only want to foster within them an association with the sea, the Navy and the merchant navy — not to form a quasi-military organisation,' he declared in an interview with the *Australian*.

David never forgot those who had helped him along the way and, accordingly, he wrote to Vice Admiral Sir David Stevenson, who had been the Executive Officer of *Vengeance*, and later Chief of Naval Staff.

Dear Admiral Stevenson,

I don't feel I can watch you retire with no more than a quick handshake in the corridor. What I'd like you to know is something like this ...

Ever since I've been in the RAN, or certainly since I was a Snottie [the nickname for Midshipmen], I've felt the benefits of your helping hand (also the occasional hot breath down my neck, gravelly cough in my ear and sharp teeth nipping my ankles). You showed an interest in me when I was in the Gunroom of *Sydney* in '51, at a time when I didn't think anyone knew I existed, then kept it up.

In *Vengeance* you found girlfriends for me, introduced me to your friends, kicked me around a bit and gave me a good deal of help and encouragement. As for foo [Fleet Operations Officer] days, I look back on them as having been rather special in a lot of ways — after the first few weeks of trauma in Bersatn Padn. Then I eventually realised that my difficulties weren't being caused by you breaking me in but by me making obstacles for myself. From then it was just happy, rewarding hard work — I throve in the trust you appeared to give me and I felt I could talk with you about anyone or anybody. And did. At all hours of the day and night. You would be startled, if not embarrassed to know how much you passed on to me by advice and example. Not least among those legacies — how trust and delegation inspires boundless loyalty, industry and respect and how friendship and care for the little people inspires devotion as well as making the donor feel good; how too much attention to the frills and trimmings — the customs rather than the traditions — is a waste of time and a constant reminder that adoring one's family strengthens a man in all ways; that it's healthy, and fun, to have as many friends as possible outside the Service; that complete honesty is practical and sensible as well as what Moses had to say about it. And a lot more, for which I'm grateful.

I've reached a very difficult age I find — not made any easier by my present task of looking at the Navy from outside it. I've always had paragons a'plenty to look up to and emulate — now I feel I've just about run out of senior Naval officers whom I want to be 'like'! I want you to know that, while I'll never try to be a carbon copy of H.D. Stevenson, I will try like hell to never forget the many lessons learnt at your knee/bridge/stool/whisky bottle/and sundry other places. If I can emulate your honest burning devotion to the job in all its aspects while, like you, never seeking promotion, I'll have more self-respect than most people could imagine possible.

So, there ye'go. I wouldn't want this to read like an In Memoriam and apologise if I have. Your friendship and frankness has done a lot for me in the past and, when I need more, I'll seek you out and come and get a transfusion. But now that you're retired I feel I have to go solo! I can't wear 'L' plates when the instructor has got out of the car.

This was just from me to you, and I'll be embarrassed if you reply so please don't. You know that my messages to Myra or Susie's to you would take as long and can be said in other ways at other times.

Good luck Sir, and thank you.
Cheers,
Dave

P.S. My Committee of Taste says this is much too bloody long but that I have a right to say what I feel!

On 16 December 1973, Captain David Martin assumed command of HMAS *Torrens*, a destroyer escort, and was also Commander of the Third Australian Destroyer Squadron, which consisted of not just one but six ships. On board, he entertained a wide range of well-known people, including the former Governor of South Australia, Sir Mark Oliphant.

Whilst commanding *Torrens*, David was astonished one day to receive a small pair of map dividers. They had been borrowed in 1941 by a young Royal Navy Petty Officer, Terry Mitchell, from his Commanding Officer in *Moresby*. When he later realised he still had them, he was in another ship and his former officer, Commander W.H. Martin, David's father, had been lost at sea. Bill Martin had lent the dividers to Mitchell when he was fixing an echo sounder on

Moresby. Mitchell was helping to train young officers in sonar and seamanship during World War II, and in 1941 was in *Moresby*, mapping strategical areas of Australian and New Guinean waters. 'Somehow they [the dividers] crept into my tool box accidentally and, long after I left the ship, I found them — I never saw Commander Martin again.' David was overjoyed to receive them, saying, 'I have very, very few heirlooms from my father because the things that Naval officers like to get — swords and medals for instance — were sunk in *Perth*'.

In February, shortly after David had been posted to *Torrens*, she served as escort to *Britannia* when Her Majesty Queen Elizabeth II toured the South Pacific. His many letters to Susie during the Royal Tour were descriptive, humorous and very frank. They were also most affectionate, just as his father's had been to his mother, many years before. 'Angel Susie Love', 'Darling Girl' and 'Sweet Susie Darling Girl', he would begin, then proceed to give a detailed description of each day's activities, complete with diagrams to prove his point and apologies for the inevitable carbon!

> ... We were due to fuel from the tanker at about 11, after Britannia had had a go, then planned to play with the anti submarine mortars in the afternoon. The Royal navigator rang me at about 9 and asked if we could change our program, and take on about half a dozen of the Household and some of the family by jackstay at 1045, give them something to look at then return them at 1215. Maybe P. Anne they said, certainly Mark. So came the first jackstay transfer with Britannia. I was only a little bit more twitched than usual!
>
> The Queen and P. Anne stood and watched as we steamed alongside and pointed their cameras at us lots. Earl Mountbatten, from 30 yards away anyway, looked terribly old. P Philip very relaxed in a beach shirt. Any'ow, it went off well. Mark came across + Admiral Sir Peter Ashmore (Master of the Royal Household) an Air Commodore (Captain of the Queen's Flight), P. Heseltine (the Australian Assistant Secretary), and 4 others including 2 Ladies in Waiting.

Apparently little Annie hates jackstays. Mark P. is a very typical pleasant army Captain — has put on a *lot* of weight since the wedding! We showed them around the ship for 25 minutes, then dragged them up top while we fired the guns and the mortars for about 10 minutes then took them all down to the wardroom at 12. Just as they settled we were told to be back alongside the Yacht at 1215, so they hadn't long to drink and chat. Also they had little chance to speak to any of the sailors while they were walking around. But they all enjoyed it …

∽

… Talked to Philip and Earl Mountbatten for a while (they did most of talking) which was interesting, particularly with P. pulling the old boy's leg a bit. Then Dickie took all the men (not Philip) and they started practicing a haka for their ship's concert coming up on Sunday. It was bloody funny. None of them young, all enjoying it and trying their best with the grunts and the thumps and cries etc., Dickie Mountbatten saying no that's no bloody good at all, we'll start again and Queen, eyes wet from laughing, going to them and showing them how to grunt better, Anne yelling encouragement to Mark. That went on for about 3/4 of an hour while the rest of us drifted around talking happily. All such a decent mob and so easy.

During this time, on 20 February 1974 to be precise, a message was sent to the Medical Officer of *Britannia* advising that there were no condoms on *Torrens* and could *Britannia* provide some assistance. They obliged. David deliberated over his response. Remembering that he had recently entertained some guests who were interested in stamps he finally despatched: 'VMT [very many thanks] supply of stores. My Philatelists will appreciate having first day covers!'

He also had his camera at the ready, recognising that his response and accompanying photo had all the earmarks of a good story for the future!

In mid-February, the Royal party came on board *Torrens*. Following the visit, David immediately wrote to Susie:

> ... Signal in the middle of the night saying programme for Thursday rearranged to allow HM, HRH, PA & MP to visit us for 20 mins, v. informally, after having the shore reception before going to lunch in Britannia! Horray. As a result we had to anchor close to the Yacht in a nasty reef circled spot which I didn't like.
>
> Any'ow, put all the sailors on the focsle [Forecastle] with no caps on, and the Family, plus the Admiral and Bill Heseltine the asst sec, came in the Royal Barge at 1120. It was heart-pumping, pulse-quickening, happy happy greet. I only introduced the 4 top officers, top CPO and PO + youngest sailor in a line then we put PA & MP up forward with No.1, PP walking around on his own and HM with me. The 20 minutes went so fast and nearly every sailor was talked to. Some were unenthusiastic about the idea at first but now ALL are comparing how many Royals they spoke to, what they said, and wasn't it the best day of the trip/of the year/in the Navy/ever. I was so so pleased. And my dear Queen was so charming and beautiful — and nice to me! A real red letter day. I was able to be a bit whimsical, some sailors bloody funny and she chatted about yesterday's flight (they had 2 goes at landing), the Yacht Concert (I think they were all surprised when Philip and I got up on the stage and joined in the first act!) and many other things too many to write.

These letters, varying from concerts to signals, were dispatched to Susie as soon as possible. A great sharer of successes and disappointments alike, David loved communicating results.

> ... Had a signal at 2 saying 'I have been commanded by Her Majesty the Queen to invite you to dinner tonight.'
>
> The two ships joined up again at about 5, and headed for Vila in the New Hebrides. I went across by boat at 7.40

feeling not very nervous! Up to Flag Officer Royal Yacht's cabin for a 15 minute chat then down to the vast royal apartments ... Earl Mountbatten drifted in and I said hello, Princess Anne who was thinking of someone else, then HM, then Philip, and each waited for me to say how are yer mate before they did anything else ... And so to dinner where I found to my horror then pleasure that the Queen had me on her right. I had a nice Lady in Waiting (actually a Woman of the Bedchamber) on the other side. For at least the first 30 minutes Queen and I just talked to each other — ships, Goons, Charles, schools, picnics, Frenchmen — and I've never struck a more direct, friendly, warm, unstuffy person. Looking beautiful and so easy and nice. Then I chatted to the W o t B for about 10 minutes and then back to my left for the rest of the meal. Sat down about 8.30 — a fish mornay, chicken bits with spuds, peas, sprouts, lettuce and apple salad; icecream with choc pep hunks in it; 1/2 glass of Mosselly and 1/2 glass of lousy port. Then a big hunk of pawpaw.

∽

... Today Sunday, Queen left the Yacht at 10 and Britannia sailed at 1010. They sent the most utterly wonderful photos of our men, steampast and cheer, and of the Royal session on the forecastle, and the sailors are THRILLED. Remarks like Gee it makes you proud to be in the Navy, and all that.

... Then came the farewell signals, which I'll enlarge to 10 foot square and frame.

FROM QUEEN TO TORRENS

Thank you for your escort. I was most impressed by the admirable way in which you carried out your duties, the smart appearance of your ship and by your steampast. My family and I were pleased to meet so many of your ship's Company at Gizo and send all on board our best good wishes. Signed Elizabeth R.

And from Flag Officer Royal Yachts:

> It has been a great pleasure to have had you in The Royal Squadron for the past 14 days, and I am most grateful to you for your very efficient support.
> Goodbye and good sailing.
> Proverbs 31 verse 29.

(which says 'Many daughters have done virtuously, but thou excelleth them all')

COR!

Then I got my visitors' book back signed Elizabeth R, Philip and Anne. So my cup of joy floweth over.

I sent careful messages to Queen and Admiral in reply, and that's that. And wasn't it all beaut?

David was away at sea in *Torrens* for a year and a half before his next posting, to the Navy Office in Canberra, where he was the Naval man in the Force Development and Analysis Section of the Strategic Policies Division. The big challenge in this role was working with civilians. He remained in Canberra until July 1978, when he was appointed Captain of HMAS *Supply*, which was based in Sydney. *Supply*, at that time, was the fleet oiler, displacing 26 000 tons fully loaded, and was the largest ship in the Royal Australian Navy. She was named after HMS *Supply* — a ship of the first fleet. As a replenishment tanker, a support vessel with a crew of 300, she supplied food as well as fuel and oil. The ship's Engineering Officer in 1978 was none other than David's old mate, 'Curly Wee' Fahey.

Life was proceeding at a good, steady pace, then in 1979, David was promoted to Commodore and made Commanding Officer of the RAN's senior ship, the aircraft carrier *Melbourne*, Flagship of the Australian Fleet. No doubt his versatility and flexibility were the reasons he was kept on the move. Wherever there was an important gap to be filled, David Martin was the right man to fill it.

During his command, *Melbourne* visited many cities, including Hobart, Wellington and Auckland. The ship exercised with other ships, both foreign and Australian, and the Fleet Air Arm was continually operating from *Melbourne* throughout this period.

The Martins had by now sold their house in Fisher, a suburb of Canberra, and moved closer to Canberra Grammar School, which William attended. When the next overseas posting came, William became a boarder at Canberra Grammar, electing not to change schools. The girls, who had now left school, moved to Victoria and lived together there. Sandy went to a government job in the Department of Defence and Anna commenced child care studies.

The Navy has a traditional mode of farewell to the relinquishing Commanding Officer of a ship — he is rowed ashore by his senior officers. For David's farewell from *Melbourne* on 5 December 1979, something very different was planned. The Executive Officer, Commander John Foster, raised the flag that launched a specially-made 'messerschmitt', with David inside, down the flightdeck. The messerschmitt was a three-wheeled bubble car fitted with mock wings, propeller and cannons. Wearing his Victorian Railways engineer's cap, David played along, and after his 'flight' along the deck, was lowered to the wharf by crane as the band played 'Those Magnificent Men in their Flying Machines'. 'Auld Lang Syne' was followed by three lusty cheers from the crew.

Well respected as a Commanding Officer, David's quirky sense of humour had made him popular with his men, from his first trip to sea as Captain, when he flew the yellow Q flag with a large black 'L' stitched on to it to announce his 'learner' status. On the ship's return journey, the 'L' was replaced with a 'P' — he was now on his 'P' plates!

As the 1980s began, David attended the Royal College of Defence Studies in London, which for senior officers is often one of the most enjoyable times of their careers. They are given the opportunity to further broaden their minds.

It was while they were in London that David's mother died, on 8 July 1980. She was sixty-nine years old. She had survived several small strokes and had been using a wheelchair, but towards the end she was bedridden, though still coherent. Everyone at the nursing home loved her. She had an attractive unit there, purchased by her generous sister-in-law Edna Little. When it became clear that she hadn't much longer to live, the nursing home rang the Martins in London, who quickly arranged a flight back to Australia. However, shortly afterwards the nursing home called again saying that she had died. In many ways Jim had had a sad, lonely life, yet she was without bitterness and totally uncomplaining. She had often stayed with David, Susie and the children and had lived with them at various times. The family all greatly respected and loved her. Will, especially, would sit with her for hours on end. Isla Estelle Martin, Jim to everyone, had set an example of dignity, acceptance and courage. She had always made sure that family values were upheld and though times were very lonely and tough for her, she bore it all with quiet strength.

At the beginning of 1981, the Martins returned to Canberra, where David was posted as Director General of Naval Manpower in the Navy Office. William became a day boy once more and joined his mother and father at their house in Griffith. Life was changing, everyone was on the move, new horizons and possibilities were opening up.

Sandy was the first to leave the nest. She married Vincenzo Emilio Bruno Di Pietro (Vince) on 13 February 1982, at the same little church in Willaura where Susie and David had exchanged their vows a quarter of a century earlier. The reception was again under a marquee on the lawn of the homestead. A Naval man? Of course! They were soon off to England to begin a similar life to that of David and Susie.

Anna, too, went to England, though on a working holiday. She stayed for two years, making ends meet by taking a variety of jobs — working in cafés and wine bars, and nannying in Ireland, England, Spain and France.

William joined the Navy as a Midshipman in 1982, aged nineteen, and with all the children away from home, Susie and David were by themselves.

Meanwhile, back in Canberra, there was exciting news. David had been promoted to Rear Admiral. He was now well and truly in the upper echelon of the Naval fraternity. He was not expecting this promotion but was delighted when it happened. Having achieved Flag

Rank, he served as Chief of Naval Personnel in the Navy Office. In this position he was responsible for the discipline, training, morale, welfare, postings, recruiting and rehabilitation of all Royal Australian Navy personnel. He also represented the Navy on all tri-service personnel committees. All Rear Admiral positions are difficult. Heads of Department are always presented with huge challenges, but Rear Admiral Martin seemed to master them all.

Then, in 1984, out of nowhere, he was appointed Flag Officer Naval Support Command in Sydney. It was a huge and demanding job, and David was responsible for all the shore establishments up and down the east coast of Australia. Admirably, he filled the position, overseeing work done at HMAS *Albatross*, the Naval Air Station, the Naval College (HMAS *Creswell*) at Jervis Bay, and all the establishments at HMAS *Penguin*, *Platypus*, *Watson*, *Kuttabul* and *Nirimba*, which closed in 1993. He revelled in the role and his duties.

'Tresco', the Navy's official Sydney residence, situated at Elizabeth Bay, and with magnificent views of Sydney Harbour, came with the job. An imposing sandstone house, it was designed and built by Colonel Thomas Rowe in 1865. Rowe was one of the fledgling colony's leading architects and he left a legacy of splendid buildings, including Sydney Hospital, the Great Synagogue and Newington College. For Tresco, he used Italian craftsmen to sculpt the sandstone terraced lawns and gardens and the frescoes on the interior walls.

In 1913, Tresco was acquired by the Commonwealth Government for £8 000. Copies of the stone lions on Nelson's Column in Trafalgar Square, London, have been added to the building to help establish the Naval character of the residence. Paintings of ships on the walls, and a dining suite, specially made at the Navy dockyard at Garden Island, and the drawing room furniture, also reflect the Naval influence. The Naval crown is carved on the back of the dining and drawing room chairs: the crown, surrounded by Australian native flowers, is printed on the fabric.

The Martins' move into this beautiful and gracious mansion represented their twenty-fifth change of address in twenty-eight years. David, apart from his demanding job, was spending an extraordinary amount of time as official Naval host at dinners, functions and receptions. At Tresco he proved to be an excellent off-the-cuff after-dinner speaker, entertaining premiers, ambassadors and officials — Tresco was a veritable government guesthouse! But the caring, friendly and courteous resident Naval staff were a great boon to Susie in catering and offering comfort to house guests. Used to doing all the planning, shopping, preparation, serving and then washing-up in her previous positions as Naval hostess, the skilled assistance was a wonderful asset as Tresco welcomed Vice-Regal guests, diplomats and heads of foreign Naval forces.

William Martin's twenty-first birthday was celebrated at Tresco in 1984. One hundred and fifty of his Naval colleagues and friends gathered for the occasion in the red-walled ballroom, the numbers and festivities recapturing the splendour of Tresco's colonial days.

There was another celebration in 1985, when Anna Martin and Michael Beaumont were married at St Peter's Church, Watsons Bay. Michael is the son of Admiral Alan Beaumont, who had been a Cadet Midshipman at the Royal Australian Naval College at the same time as David.

Following the ceremony, the newlyweds travelled up the harbour in the Admiral's barge, alighted at the steps at the bottom of Tresco where the wedding reception was held within a marquee in the grounds.

David Martin, now in his mid-fifties, was enjoying all that the 1980s offered. Changes were afoot. He invariably welcomed a challenge and was receptive to new directions. 'Always Ready', the family motto, applied to him — especially if such directions were near, on, in, over, or at his beloved sea. To him, the sea represented humanity. It typified the world, highlighting human endeavour. A world sometimes calm, sometimes merciless. In fact, he had often expressed the opinion that a nation's capital should be intimately linked with the environs of the sea. The ocean, being so vast and possessing such grandeur, has a humbling effect. Humankind is often at the mercy of the elements. The sea influences our work, our play and our view of the world. As Canberra is inland, he often quipped, 'No wonder politicians see a superficial world rather than reality'.

CHAPTER SEVEN

SEVENTY-FIFTH ANNIVERSARY CELEBRATION

A beaut birthday bash — which lasted a week!

Ken Swain first met David Martin in 1974 when Ken was posted to *Torrens* as Communications Officer. David was Captain, Commander of the Third Australian Destroyer Squadron.

Usually, only Squadron Commanders and Admirals have specialist Communications Officers — there are simply not enough of them to go around. Ken was the specialist on board *Torrens*. On Ken's first day, David welcomed him, saying, 'Good, Ken, I've never had a Communications Officer before. In addition to all your normal duties, I'd like you to come up with about one thousand Biblical quotations suitable for Captains to communicate with each other.' After Ken had recovered from the shock, he availed himself of both the Old and New Testaments, and every night went to bed with Genesis, Chapter 4, Verse 6 on his mind. All the stewards referred to him as the 'bible-bashing bastard'. Nothing could have been further from the truth!

The book of quotations was duly produced and extensively used, never more so than to and from Flag Officer Royal Yacht, during the Royal Tour of the South Pacific. 'Perhaps a certain amount of one-upmanship was involved in the exercise,' says Ken Swain, 'but it made the men sharp, proud and caring. It kept both the men and the game alive.' Rituals and superstitions are commonplace in the Navy. Proverbs were used widely and freely. David had his own examples, which he provided to all concerned.

Occasion	Ref	Text
Blast	John 16–21	I have yet many things to say unto you but ye cannot bear them now
Ordering junior ships to detach	Proverbs 20–26	A wise king scattereth the wicked, and bringeth the wheel over them
Diving operations	Proverbs 20–23	Diver's weights are an abomination unto the Lord, and a false balance is not good
To an uncommunicative junior ship	Isaiah 29–15	Woe unto them that seek deep to hide their counsel from the Lord, and their works are in the dark and they say 'Who seeth us?' and 'who knoweth us?'

These were duly signed by D.J. Martin, Captain.

In addition to proverbs, the Navy has a vocabulary all its own. Bravo Zulu means 'well done', PSB stands for 'please send boat'. One is never offered 'another drink' (which implies you have already had one); instead, 'the other half' is proffered and poured. 'Scran' is a Naval word for food, and 'horse's neck' is a term used for brandy and dry. Pink gins and gin and ice are the order of the day! Everyone seems to understand such language and abbreviations easily.

Ken Swain had come from HMAS *Stuart* before joining the more modern *Torrens*. He was thrilled to be on board for four months, during which time 'We followed the Royal Yacht around to every single island where there was a white ex-pat Brit. We'd pull in, haul the flag up in exotic places like Pentecost and the Solomon Islands, have cocktail parties till we were sick of them ... and this went on for three weeks. The highlight of the trip — for everyone — was when David Martin received a personal invitation to dine with the Queen.'

'Whatever time I come back tonight, I'm not in command of the ship', was his farewell instruction to the Executive Officer, realising that the Queen would offer him a drink, which he would accept. He returned at 11 pm and Ken Swain was the Officer on Watch on the Bridge.

'Everyone was bursting to know how the evening had gone, but we kept quiet as the Captain always makes the first move or says the first word.' Finally the silence was too much for Ken: 'Come on, Sir, tell us all about it'. With a beam, David replied, 'I thought nobody would ever ask', then spoke enthusiastically for over an hour.

According to Ken, 'You work for some Captains because you like them and you'd hate to see the Admiral or the Captain "get in the soup". You're doubly careful, you work twice as hard. Others get the job done through discipline — they *make* you work rather than you *want* to work — but with David Martin it was the former because of his personality and the care he exercised.'

Although Ken Swain was promoted to Commander in June 1979, he decided to leave the Navy in 1980. When he'd first joined as an eighteen-year-old sailor, he knew he'd leave at forty-two. He loved the sea, had wanted to see the world and couldn't afford it, and for an Able Seaman to reach Commander status, he'd done very well indeed. He'd worked very hard and had been promoted steadily. To Ken, the Navy was like playing snakes and ladders, but there were many more ladders than snakes. Everything was spelled out clearly; it was obvious that if you succeeded at one thing then another would occur. He saw it as a blueprint for life, and although he 'loved the Navy through and through', he was off 'to make a million dollars'.

So, despite having been second-in-command of HMAS *Yarra* — a rare achievement for a sailor — he was business bent and became 'Kenny the Corer'! 'Have your lawn looking like a bowling green', he advertised. The first weekend he got twenty jobs. And they continued. Four hundred dollars per weekend boring holes in lawns was a hundred more than his weekly pay as a Naval Lieutenant. He soon had three people working for him. It was then that he made a startling discovery: 'You never get rich working for a boss, you get richer working for yourself and you get very rich having someone work for you'. He stresses that money itself is not important — it's the achievement that counts.

When he sold his coring business, he got a real estate licence and diploma; then, after working for a large company, began his own real estate business. Ken Swain liked these five-yearly challenges.

One day in July 1985, much to his surprise, Ken received a call from the Navy, inviting him to do one month's Reserve Training in Canberra. When he went for the interview he was informed that his was one of three names submitted to Admiral Martin, who had to select a person to co-ordinate the Seventy-fifth Anniversary Celebration of the Royal Australian Navy in 1986.

'We want someone who is bloody alive,' said David when they met, 'not half dead.'

'What could I do?' asked Ken.

'We want this big birthday party to reach out to everyone. It will be the first major Fleet Review. It's not just an internal thing. It's a case of the Royal Australian Navy saluting the nation.'

'Well, I'm used to knocking on doors. Could I ask, say, the Commonwealth Bank for sponsorship?'

'We've never done anything like that before ... sponsorship! Hang on a minute and I'll ring Mike Hudson [Chief of Naval Support] and get the Minister's approval,' replied David.

Kim Beazley, then Minister for Defence, gave the nod.

Ken Swain took the job. Recalled to full-time duty, he had an opportunity to do things he'd never done before. His challenge: to put the Navy that he loved with the deepest of emotions on the map. In doing so, it would introduce him to a different echelon and a whole range of new skills. It was also the end of his five-year plan, so he was ready for the challenge. Not least, David Martin would be great to work for, he would not be a 'crusty old Admiral'.

Between the two of them, this was going to be the birthday bash of all time. Each man was as excited and enthusiastic as the other. David introduced Ken to Sir Asher Joel, head of the Asher Joel Media Group, who had been responsible for the Captain Cook Bicentenary, and had organised the first Papal visit to Australia and the opening of the Sydney Opera House. The great entrepreneur. Sir Asher immediately offered one hour of his time each week, wherever he was, for the next nine months. 'I want no rubbish — tell me what your problems are around town,' he said.

When Ken went to see him in the first week and said, 'I don't know whether the Governor-General is going to take the Salute — it may take months before we receive an answer', Sir Asher reached for the phone and dialled.

'Hello, Ninian. How's everyone? ... Yes, the Navy. Well, I'll book you in from 12 to 3 pm so they can do with you what they will. Details later.' Mission accomplished. It was the same with the Lord Mayor.

'Hello, Doug ... lunch with [hand over phone] how many?'

'One hundred and fifty', mouthed Ken.

'Three hundred', Sir Asher told the Mayor. Done.

'What is Wran doing for you?' he asked Ken. Ken shook his head.

'Hello, Neville ... State Reception ... 500 people. Details later.'

There were still five minutes of the hour left.

'Anyone else?'

'Not today thank you, Sir Asher', whispered Ken. Time for that week was up. The assistance and friendship which began in 1985 continues to this day.

Protocol and procedure were handled with the same enthusiasm and excellence. It took a year's preparation to organise the celebration. The Navy's public relations budget was $17 000 for the year. To Ken's request for more, he received the following letter:

> Based on previous years and notwithstanding the size of the 75th Anniversary, it is not expected that the budget needs to exceed $17 000.

It ended up costing $1.8 million. Over one million dollars was obtained from publicity and donations in kind. Corporations responded to the call and opened their minds and wallets — there were videos, voice-overs, commercials, slides, lectures and speaking engagements. David and Ken were like two kids in a lolly shop. Together they made it happen. David with his leadership qualities guided them both and Ken worked round the clock. The Bond Corporation, Four X, Tooheys, and Swan Brewery in the United States all answered the sponsorship call.

'What do you want?' asked Bill Widerberg, Chief Executive Officer of the Bond Brewing Division.

'$100 000 for advertising, $200 000 for fireworks, $50 000 for a wraparound on the *Daily Telegraph* on the day. Total $350 000.'

'You've got it', came the answer from Widerberg.

It was, of course, the 1980s!

Then came the next question.

'Ken, what have you got going in 1988?'

'We've got the spectacular Naval Salute as part of the Bicentennial celebrations — sixty-three ships from all round the world and 23 000 sailors, Prince Andrew and Fergie. They've asked me to stay on.' By now Kenny the Corer was gone, Michael Edgley was more his style.

David and Ken — both of whom were hell-bent on public relations and promotion for the celebration — agreed that they must try to get on every radio station and television channel possible so they could spread the word about the Seventy-fifth Anniversary to Australia at large. David went on Channel Nine's national 'Today' show and was asked the question, 'With all these foreign ships and submarines coming, I suppose it will be inevitable that some of them will be carrying nuclear weapons?' Intending to say 'It is not inevitable', he left out the vital word 'not'. He went on with the interview, but as soon as he returned to the office that morning he summoned Ken Swain.

'Ken, I think I've blown it.'

The telephone rang constantly. Their wish had been granted. They certainly were on every radio and television program! There

*The redoubtable Esther Abrahams
(1771–1846)*

*The gallant George Johnston
(1764–1823)* (Image Library, State
Library of New South Wales)

Jim and Bill in Cornwall, England

Jim and David

Bill and David

David with 'Lanky', his good friend the rabbit

David, aged 8, with close friend Bill Hunter

David James Martin in his Scots College uniform

In the swimming pool at Flinders Naval Depot: David is sixth from the front

Three generations of Martin Cadet Midshipmen: Bill, David and William

David and Susie on their wedding day, 1957

Three little Martins: Anna, William and Sandy, London, 1965

David greets Sir Mark Oliphant on board HMAS Torrens, *1974*

Her Majesty, Queen Elizabeth, and HRH Prince Philip, the Duke of Edinburgh being welcomed on board Torrens, *1974*

Terry Mitchell and David with the returned dividers, 1974

Susie and David during HMAS Melbourne's *visit to Hobart, 1979*

A flying farewell from HMAS Melbourne, *1979* (RAN ©)

A spectacular Sydney salute: the RAN's Seventy-fifth Anniversary, 1986 (RAN ©)

USS Missouri *helps Sydney celebrate, 1986* (RAN ©)

Father of the Year luncheon, 1988
(back, l–r) Michael Beaumont, William Martin, David, Vince Di Pietro
(front, l–r) Anna Beaumont, Susie, Sandy Di Peitro

Retirement day, 1988 (RAN ©)

Sarah Adams, Wayne Wilkinson (Project Manager), David, Susie and Lieutenant Colin Bold, inspecting the Sydney Harbour Tunnel Project, 1990

Benji Martin: watchdog extraordinaire

Father Christmas and his helpers

Farewell wishes from the entire staff of Government House, August 1990

A fond farewell, 16 August 1990

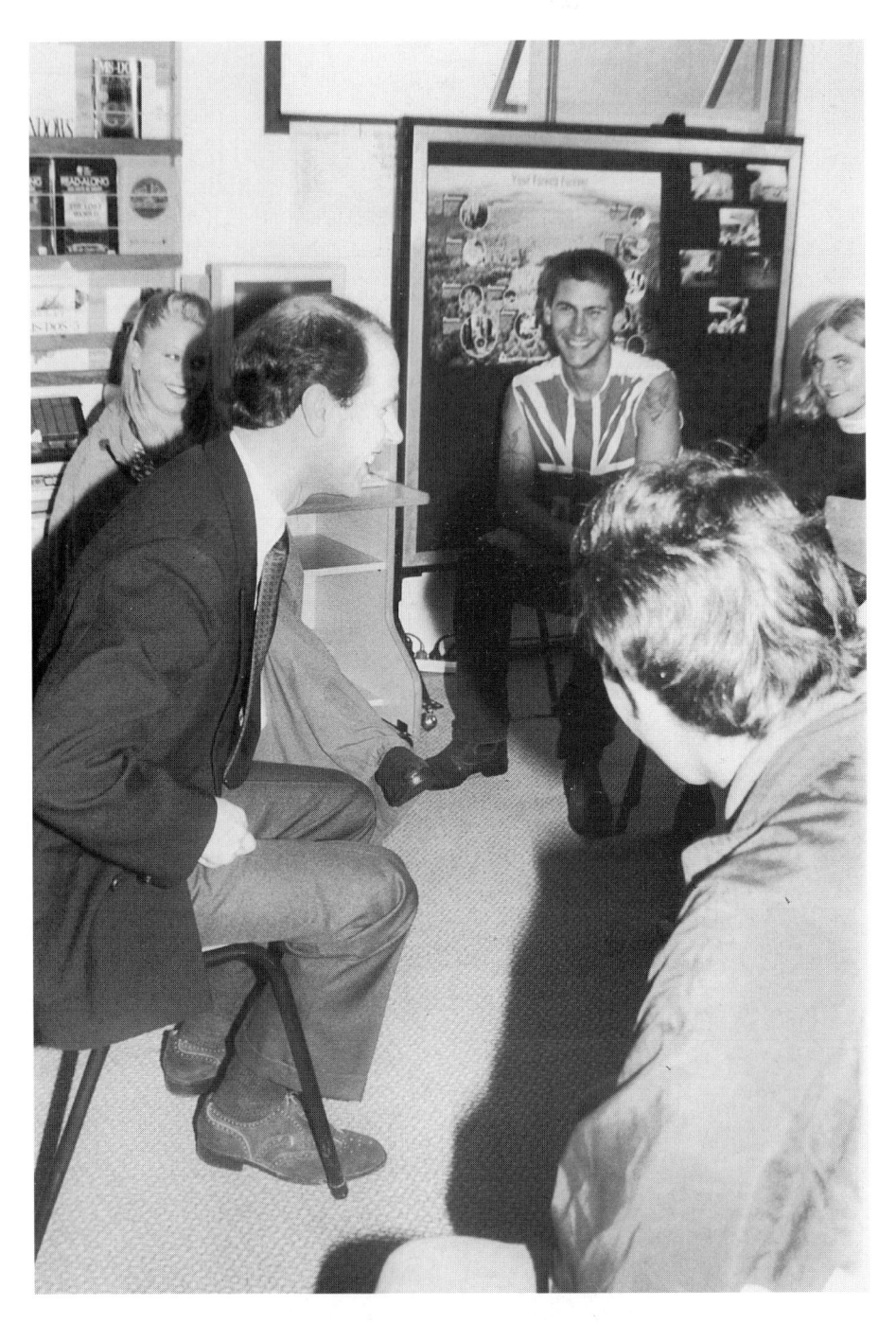

Prince Edward at Triple Care Farm, March 1994
(Sir David Martin Foundation)

were thirty-two interviews that day alone. It was red-hot news. David was blasted by Kim Beazley. The rumours varied from 'David Martin is sacked' to 'David Martin is hung, drawn and quartered', even from his friend and boss, Vice Admiral Michael Hudson, who had joined the Navy in the same intake as David.

David admitted he'd made a mistake, claiming he was nervous and unused to doing national television interviews — especially early in the morning — and, turning a minus into a plus, the media got behind him and proclaimed, 'Hooray, an honest Admiral!'.

In 1979, David had also managed to turn a potential disaster into a PR opportunity. Ken Swain was the Fleet Communications Officer on the Flag Bridge of *Melbourne*, there was a howling gale off the New South Wales coast, and the aircraft, an A4, worth a million dollars, was not tied down.

Captain David Martin roared, 'Quick, we've got to turn', and the Deck Officer warned, 'Sir, we haven't strapped down the aircraft yet'. David replied, 'It's not that rough — it'll be okay'. They turned course. In the huge swell, the million-dollar aircraft rolled over and went sliding off the ship — with a sailor in it. Fortunately there was a Rescue Destroyer coming up behind and in thirty seconds the sailor was plucked out of the sea. Quick as a flash, David got his public relations man on board to film the mountainous seas, describing it as 'the worst particular day we've ever seen in the New South Wales coast' and saying, 'Weren't we fortunate to lose only one aircraft instead of several?'. He then got a helicopter to take the footage to all the commercial television stations. After watching television that evening, the nation as a whole thought, 'Thank goodness we didn't lose the whole fleet!'.

David rarely sought publicity, but regarded the media as his friends, so if ever anything needed to be explained or sorted out, he'd give them a call. It always worked.

Ken Swain had been particularly busy about a month before the Seventy-fifth Anniversary Celebration. He had ambassadors, the Duke of Edinburgh, Ministers and the Prime Minister to worry about. The Prime Minister, Bob Hawke, had declined the invitation to attend the celebration. Ken had then sent him a telegram and was anxious that David knew about it.

Sir,

1. I wish to advise you that I forwarded the attached telegram to the Prime Minister of Australia last Thursday evening, 25 September 1986.

2. My reasons for taking this unusual step are self-explanatory, as indicated in the telegram. I wish to emphasise this action was dictated by the very best motives because I feel deeply and sincerely, both as a citizen and Emergency List Naval Officer, that the wonderful occasion of the Naval Review would be enhanced by the presence of the Prime Minister. I further emphasise that the telegram was sent as Mr Ken Swain, Australian citizen, urging his Prime Minister to attend an event of great pageantry and significance to the Royal Australian Navy and to the Australian people.

3. Apart from the obvious non-conformity to the usual Service methods of communication, the only minor problem which may arise is the question of cost. If anyone should query this, the telegram was sent from my home telephone number at a cost of $56.90, which has been charged to my personal telephone account. No cost was incurred to the Navy.

4. I do not regret forwarding the telegram, however I will be most upset if I cause you any embarrassment whatsoever over this matter.

TEXT OF TELEGRAM SENT TO PM 25 SEPTEMBER 1986

Sir,

I have just been advised that you will not be attending the Naval Review to be conducted by HRH The Duke of Edinburgh in Sydney on 4 October. If this is so may I express my personal disappointment and request you reconsider using the following points of which you may be unaware as the basis for my request:

1. 41 Allied warships from 7 nations will be present.
2. 8,000 visiting sailors and 5,000 Australian sailors will participate.
3. In excess of 5,000 ex-Naval personnel will be in attendance.
4. The harbour foreshores will be lined with in excess of 100,000 Australians.
5. The harbour will be filled by thousands of small craft.
6. The event will be televised live and be of a magnitude rarely seen in this country.
7. Your non-attendance could be seen as a snub to the 15,000 members of the Royal Australian Navy and the many thousands more ex-Naval personnel who served this country in war and peace for 75 years.

I forward this communication not as a serving Naval officer but as an Australian citizen who believes his Prime Minister should devote three hours of his valuable time to celebrate the Navy's 75th Anniversary Celebration. May I take the liberty of suggesting the exposure would certainly do you no harm.

Commander K.A. Swain
Co-ordinator RAN 75th Anniversary Celebration

Needing some reassurance, Ken approached David, whose door was always open, and anxiously enquired, 'Boss, may I see you?'.

'Sorry, Ken — in half an hour.'

'No, Boss, this is important.'

'Half an hour, Ken.'

Impatiently Ken wondered what could be more important than his dilemma. Then he found out — an Able Seaman had just been admitted to hospital. David had gone immediately to see him and to have a word with his wife. On his return half an hour later, he said, 'Okay, Ken, where were we?'. This is a fine example of how David always put people before projects. He was humane and compassionate. That's just the way he was.

David read the telegram carefully. He pursed his lips before he responded, 'This is very serious, Ken'. The Prime Minister obviously thought so too. He came.

After many months of planning, the big week of celebration finally arrived. They came from all over the world for the party: Britain, Canada, the United States, France, New Zealand and Papua New Guinea. The Royal Australian Navy had proudly brought its mates home — eight thousand of them. The most heavily escorted had been the American vessels. Over the preceding weeks, protesters had launched a growing campaign against the possible presence of nuclear weapons in Sydney Harbour, and had indicated that they were going to turn their words into waterborne action. For their part, the police and members of the public who were there to welcome the Americans had been equally determined that there would be no halt in the Fleet entry. And, in a colourful variety of small craft, both sides had taken to the water.

After all, the main purposes of the celebration were to allow the people of Australia to share in the Navy's Seventy-fifth Anniversary: to demonstrate to the public, in a peaceful and persuasive manner, the importance of sea power in Australia and to alert politicians and influential persons to the need, and therefore the need for funds, for a viable Navy to protect Australia's coastline.

At Mrs Macquarie's Chair, the best vantage point opposite the berthing area, protesters and greeters intermingled. And the antinuclear lobby didn't entirely have its own way.

HMS *Illustrious* swept in as the jewel of the British Task Group. With a full carrier air group and an admirable staff, the ship's complement was about 1 100 officers and sailors, all of whom were determined to have some fun in the Sydney sun.

As for *Missouri*, David Martin stated, 'We hadn't particularly asked for *Missouri*, the US Navy decided to send her as their leading emissary for this party. She's big, she's a novelty for Australia. We hadn't had a battleship here since World War II. *Missouri* was the ship in which the formal surrender was signed on 2 September 1945, bringing to a close WWII'.

When the 58 000 tonne battleship anchored, she immediately became the prime focus of attention. Our highly decorated Naval Commanders and Captains played host to thousands of retired Australian Navy veterans, the old and bold, all eager to tread *Missouri*'s historic decks and exchange stories of life at sea. Everyone wanted a close look at those sixteen-inch guns.

As part of the celebration, there had been one of the largest parades Sydney had ever seen. Two and a half thousand men and bands from seven nations had taken part. It had been a day of glitter and ceremony. Crowds had gathered in the sunshine all along the route. They packed the Town Hall where the Governor-General, Sir Ninian Stephen, took the salute. With him, to honour the White Ensign, was an array of civilian dignitaries and admirals. The Navy and the city had joined hands in welcome. The Royal Marine Band from the British contingent was resplendent in leopard skin and scarlet stripes, symbolic of centuries of battles at sea. Prince Philip, Duke of Edinburgh, on board HMAS *Cook*, was the Reviewing Officer for what can best be described as a spectacular sequence of military pomp and pagentry, rarely seen in Australia. Massive warships firing salutes, military bands on all main vantage points and a major flypast of many of the world's most sophisticated military aircraft. At dusk, most of Sydney's ferries and small craft quietly took up positions around the Opera House, Harbour Bridge and other harbour viewing points. There was barely room to manoeuvre, and the setting was perfect.

Following the parade, the ships moved into position for the Review. The purpose of a Review either at sea or on shore has always been to gather all the ships departing or returning from a great campaign. It dates back to the Crusades and the Middle Ages. The first recorded Royal Review was staged in 1415 for King Henry V as he sailed to battle with France. The last one in Sydney Harbour had been recorded a quarter of a century ago. Now, in 1986, forty-two warships, the largest peacetime armada ever to gather in Sydney Harbour, had manoeuvred for a great event. *Illustrious* launched its full complement of helicopters and sea harriers.

The crowd was given an incredible display, rather like a Naval battle, with 1 700 separate shells being fired from six barges. Fireworks cascaded from Sydney's famed Harbour Bridge for the first time. Prince Philip arrived on the RAN Flagship HMAS *Stalwart* to view the spectacle.

Sydney had been the best place in the world to have a Review of this type, because it has so many splendid vantage points. Everyone had been so close to the action that they had felt they were part of it; they could touch it and smell it and see it.

The day following the Review, all foreign and Australian warships were 'open for public inspection'. Neither David nor Ken had anticipated such a massive public response to see the ships, particularly *Missouri*. They had planned very carefully for a crowd of about 150 000, using the combined size of capacity crowds at the Melbourne and Sydney Cricket Grounds as a guide. They added another 10 per cent and thought, 'We can't possibly expect any more than that'.

An additional 100 000 people came and at least 100 000 more were turned away. Thanks to good luck rather than good management, a potential crowd control disaster was averted. This crowd control aspect greatly assisted the authorities planning for Australia's Bicentennial Celebrations.

When the Seventy-fifth Anniversary Celebration of the Royal Australian Navy was completed, David drew up a list headed 'Hits and Misses'. The former was considerably longer than the latter!

1. Hits

a The Navy, without outside assistance, co-ordinated a series of spectacular events such as rarely seen in this country.

b. The Navy projected to the Australian people, in a persuasive way, the diplomatic strength of sea power.

c. The messages of the anti-military and anti-nuclear lobby were put into perspective by the public and were largely ignored.

d. Australians showed public pride in THEIR Navy not experienced in WWII.

e. Visiting personnel, many of them very senior, were impressed by the RAN's capability to stage a most impressive event. The smooth command, control, co-ordination and implementation did not go unnoticed by our visitors.

f. Morale and confidence in Fleet and Support Command personnel lifted, at least for the time being.

g. An excellent working relationship was established with many State Government Ministers, senior public servants, Police, MSB, DMR, Department of Aviation, and a wide cross-section of State and Local Government personnel.

h. Perhaps for the first time for many years, the Navy put a human face to the corporate sector and general public, and showed its professionalism and integrity.

i. New Public Relations methods and attitudes were tried and were successful, which led to positive help and support from the media.

j. Federal, State and Local Government representatives took note and were impressed.

k. The public showed that defence is an interesting topic; the traditional apathy was swept away.

2. Misses

a. The crowd control on the Sunday at Garden Island was serious and could have been disastrous.

b. Because of the money and manpower available, too many Naval people had to work much too hard. In the transport section (because civilian over-time had not been budgeted for) Naval drivers were employed for 14/16 hours per day to meet transport deadlines — this is not an isolated example.

c. Much of the day to day business in the Fleet and Support Command suffered because of the need to neglect some routine activities.

d. Inadequate telephone facilities in the CIC caused lengthy delays to some operational matters and hampered many hospitality arrangements.

But whatever David's thoughts on the matter, the letters that flooded in spoke volumes. From Commodore Dechaineux came the following message:

Dear Brave Dave,

What a weekend — bloody marvellous!

Please accept my congratulations for a superb job — I cannot begin to tell you how many people have commented on the great display that the Navy put on — I am very proud, and the Navy can be well pleased. Clearly, the best thing since sliced bread.

Mo and I took the family down to GI to see the fireworks after the review and they were ecstatic with praise — I hope Bondy got some good tucker that night!!!

A ripper Dave — many BZs
Pete

P.S. A little bit of nonsense attached.

> The 4th of October was Navy's day
> A Birthday party — hip hip hooray
> The ships they came from near and far
> Little boats, big boats and jolly jack tar
> The Yanks were there with Mighty Mo

Guns a'bristling (with nukes below)
New Zealand on the far harbour side
And the Froggies slipped in on the morning tide
Phil the Duke reviewed the fleet
And many were those he chanced to meet
Bob was there (Phil's shadow I thought)
And the 1st SL resplendent and taut
Brave Dave of whom we all are proud
Doffed his hat to the eager crowd
But I couldn't tell from my vantage on rocks
Whether he was wearing red and green socks!

The Minister for Defence, Kim Beazley, appreciated 'the monumental task' and passed on his thanks and appreciation.

Dear Admiral Martin,

I would like to congratulate you and your staff for all the organisation behind the marvellous week of celebrations and activities to mark the 75th Anniversary of the Royal Australian Navy.

Mary and I thought that the performance of the Combined Bands of the Royal Australian Navy was superb and only surpassed by the Fleet Review and the excellent fireworks display. The organisational problems for these events and the support of visiting ships must have been a monumental task. However, I am sure that the smoothness with which the week flowed and the support and involvement shown by the people of Sydney was well worth the months of planning.

Please pass my thanks and congratulations on to all members of your staff involved in the behind the scenes planning.

Yours sincerely
Kim Beazley

As David summed it up: 'For the Royal Australian Navy this has been a time for reflection, thanksgiving, dedication, celebration and very hard work. We have been striving to promote the Navy and to explain the importance of sea-power for preserving peace and protecting Australia.'

He also summed up his own feelings about the year: 'A kaleidoscope of excitement, atmosphere and events'.

It had been what they had hoped for. A party that had stopped Sydney. A beaut birthday bash — which lasted a week!

CHAPTER EIGHT

A Short Retirement

Thank you, but it doesn't really sound like me

From 1985 to 1988, Admiral David Martin had been in the thick of everything worth mentioning in the state of New South Wales. The Martins had certainly held the focus; all had revolved around their activities. Now was the perfect time for David to retire. Following the magnificent bicentenary of the first settlement in Sydney on Australia Day, 26 January 1988, and his planning of the events for the year, the scene had been securely set. There was no better time to go than now, whilst on an absolute high.

He reflected on his long and illustrious Naval career — a career which had spanned more than four decades. There had been many voyages, rough weather, high seas and intolerable conditions. There had been fear and danger, with midnight anti-smuggling patrols. His career had progressed and spiralled through the ranks — Commander, Rear Admiral, Chief of Naval Personnel, and finally Flag Officer Naval Support Command. He was one of the most senior men in Australia's Senior Service. In recent times positions at Tresco were held for approximately eighteen months but, to the delight of all and the envy of many, the Martins were there for four full, happy, stimulating years.

David had been offered a posting to Washington D.C. as Head of Australian Defence Staff. This posting was discussed at length at a family conference. He balanced the pros and cons. He carefully considered the appointment, then declined. He resigned from the Royal Australian Navy in February 1988, just two months before his fifty-fifth birthday. Enough was enough.

David viewed retirement as another step forward — certainly not sideways or backwards. He thought of it as exciting, just another move, but this time only five minutes away from Elizabeth Bay to Cameron Street, Edgecliff.

There were no regrets, only good things to look forward to — more time for his children and grandchildren, more fun with Susie, a smaller house and the opportunity to do lots of things he had been forced to put on hold. He wanted to be as private as possible, toss away all the suitcases from previous travels and never move again. He wanted a job 'doing something worthwhile with decent people'.

To celebrate, he had a surprise for his wife of thirty years. He arrived home one day declaring, 'I've had your car registered — do you want to come and see it?' 'No,' said Susie, 'no need to *see* it, thank you.' A short time later, he mentioned it again. Once more Susie said thank you and remained where she was. Finally, he could wait no longer and, talking her hand, he led her into the driveway, where there was a bright red car with a brand new number plate — BUN 200. His pet name for her was 'Bunny' (her nickname from school) and the importance of 200 in the year 1988 spoke for itself. She loved it and drives it proudly to this day.

David had always liked giving and receiving gifts. This dated right back to the time when he and Susie had met on board *Orcades*, and he took three days to select and spend the huge sum of £7 on a powder compact for her at the ship's shop. She was the same, always seeking to surprise him with interesting, imaginative and fun things. They were both very good at it. Neither of them was materialistic. They liked gifts to give pleasure and rarely overspent. David disliked waste of any kind and always looked for how to save money rather than spend it. He wasn't mean — indeed, he was most generous — but he was careful. His mother had been poor and he had always been on a wage.

Both Susie and David were in excellent spirits and in good health, though David had to wear a hearing aid. Nearly all Gunnery

Officers lose their hearing to some degree because of the years they spend training without wearing earplugs. He had always made an effort to keep fit and well. When living in Canberra, David used to cycle, and in London he would power-walk to work and change into a suit once he arrived there.

Rear Admiral Martin's last day in the Navy, 5 February 1988, dawned bright and clear. His had been a career of innovation, organisation and leadership which led to major achievements. His forty-year association with the Navy ended with the customary Change of Command ceremony. However, in this case, the traditional departure by row boat was discarded in favour of a gun carriage borne by his fellow officers and flanked by a platoon of sailors in tricorn hats. The thirteen-gun salute, cheers and rousing applause confirmed David's popularity with all ranks. He was succeeded by Rear Admiral Horton as Naval Support Commander.

That same day there was there was more fun, laughter and balloons at the Naval Supplies Centre at Zetland. More than two thousand officers and sailors were there from *Kuttabul, Nirimba, Waterhen, Penguin* and *Watson*. It was a warm and wonderful farewell, a great recognition of outstanding service.

'My whole life in the Navy has been terrific — the people, the places, the work are all memorable. When you get on a ship, despite rank and all of that, it is impossible to big-note yourself,' he told the crowd. 'My basic memory of the Navy is of being in a ship verging on the dangerous but being confident that your colleagues would not let you down. There is no room for a bludger or for someone with bad breath, no room for the fellow who can't fit in.'

David Martin retained the Naval man's capacity for companionability (you're lost without it on a ship), generosity (shipmates share), and that indefatigable propensity for a good time (but only after the job at hand was done). Fun was a byword in his prepared and private pronouncements — the fun which could be expressed as an essential part of mental wellbeing, the fun of 'hard yakka' in sport or work, and the exhilaration of serving his country for more than forty years. He left his bucket behind him with the Royal Australian Navy, saying, 'I have always been seasick — Captains can have their own buckets'.

On his last day, David received from Sir Asher Joel a letter paying respect 'to one who has attained and served with distinction such distinguished rank.'

> Dear Admiral Martin,
>
> As this will be my last letter to you as Flag Officer, Naval Support Command, I felt that perhaps I should address it in more formal terms than usual and in accordance with the precedence set out in Australian Protocol & Procedures.
>
> As a humble RANVR Lieutenant (retired), may I pay my respects to one who has attained and served with distinction such distinguished Rank.
>
> Having been engulfed myself for the past forty-three years in the maelstrom of seavil life, as distinct from service life, I seek your indulgence and pray your forgiveness for any presumption for the remarks I am about to make on this the significant occasion of your honourable retirement.
>
> At all times I have found you in every respect ready for sea, prepared to engage the enemy and to proceed safely to your destination. You have navigated many uncharted waters and your ETA has consistently been on time. Your arrival has always been notable because of your flair for courtesy and in the exchanging of salutes. Your gifts of bright beads and the good times you have brought with you to the hostile natives, whom incidentally you are now about to join, have earned the wholehearted appreciation of the recipients of your bounty.
>
> Throughout your career you have been fortunate to have had as your Executive Officer, Susie, that great Volunteer Reserve Member upon whom you will find the need for even greater reliance in the future to ensure that not only are your ETAs on time, but your ETDs also.
>
> As in the case of all males who exchange uniform for the drab suits of commerce, industry and the social milieu, you

will now find that your Executive Officer may well assume Command. A well deserved promotion, if I may be bold enough to forward my own personal recommendation to the authorities concerned.

Finally, Sir, please accept with the utmost sincerity the above comments as an expression of the affection and appreciation of one Junior and his own Commanding Officer — Asher and Sybil Joel — for the gift of your friendship and gratitude for your personal contribution to our country through the Senior Service which in our respective ways we have been so proud to serve.

May you proceed to your future destinations with all speed and God's blessings.

At the end of his last day, it was farewell to Tresco where he and Susie had been so happy. They stayed for two nights at The Sebel of Sydney, just around the corner, whilst they caught their breath before moving to Edgecliff.

Since Tresco had been so beautifully equipped, the Martins' furniture had been in storage. On reassessing it, they decided they'd have a garage sale, since most of it now seemed unsuitable. A smart car cruised by and a woman got out whilst the driver parked. It only took ten seconds before she exclaimed, 'That rubbish! I've got better than that at home', and yelled to the retreating car, 'Don't worry about parking, Fred, it's all garbage here!' and left. David and Susie looked at each other and laughed, agreeing that it was 'mostly garbage'.

They set about painting their new house, and spent some time in their little garden, which they loved. David fancied himself as a handyman, but Susie recalls, 'he was not always successful with chisels, hammers, nails and things'. Everything was 'difficult': he never seemed to have the right equipment, he'd wobble on something, or fall off, and things would break. He could change a washer, wheel a wheelbarrow and mix cement, but the projects he undertook weren't always lasting! In fact, the family coined the phrase 'doing a Davo', which meant things not working as well as they should, despite all the paraphernalia in the world!

The 1980s had been sensational years for David. In addition to everything else, in 1985 he was awarded the Order of Australia for service to the Royal Australian Navy, particularly as Chief of Naval Personnel.

In retirement, he was in no hurry for a new challenge. He was enjoying taking stock of his life — the right job would come at the right time. Within a few weeks, it had. The Premier's Department telephoned, inviting him to come in to meet with the Honourable Nick Greiner. He took the train from Edgecliff into the city, thinking 'it may be a good job with the Railways'. On his return home, he was beaming, and excitedly he told Susie, 'It's the big one'.

David was extremely proud to have been invited to consider the recommendation by the Premier to Her Majesty the Queen for the position of Governor of New South Wales.

Governor. Representing the Queen. His Sovereign. Yes!

The Martins were sworn to secrecy until the time the announcement was made much later in the year. It was then Easter, 1988. How could they contain themselves for so long? Many of their friends and associates began to telephone, advising David of positions they'd heard about which may suit. His response to all their suggestions was, 'Thank you, but it doesn't really sound like me', which surprised them, since these positions could only be described as very decent jobs with salaries which were even more decent.

Then, in the latter part of 1988, after the announcement was made, he received a Knighthood — Knight Commander of the Order of St Michael and St George (KCMG). Membership of the ancient order, which was instituted in 1818, is conferred on those who may render or who have rendered extraordinary and important services. All David's family and relatives attended Admiralty House for the investiture, including Aunt Edna and Uncle Roy whom David had been calling by their first names since a young lad. Then well in their eighties, they were extremely proud of their nephew's latest achievement. No doubt Esther and George were present in spirit. Sir Ninian Stephen, Governor-General of Australia, dubbed him Sir David. Susie was surprised that only one shoulder (the left) was dubbed — she'd always believed it was on both!

Some time later they gathered together to discuss, devise and draw up the family Coat of Arms. This heraldic emblem and personal insignia would be hung in the main hall at Government House and would also be engraved into the wall outside on the colonnades. It was a great honour for them all and, being a united family, everyone had to have a say. They finally settled on David's mother's family motto — *Sans Tache* (Without Stain) and recognised Susie's (as well as his mother's) family background in the rural industry with a merino sheep. The Southern Cross was featured, too. The Navy, of course, was not forgotten and Britannia ruled supreme. Finally, they were all satisfied. It was only later when the final proof, presented in a magnificent box, came to Government House for approval that members of staff looked at it. Closely. It was the positioning of the cannon in relation to the ram which caused a bit of a problem. They all noticed it at the same moment, exchanged a quick look with each other and agreed 'It'll have to go back to the drawing board'.

David Martin was the first Governor to come from the ranks of the Royal Australian Navy, and the last to be knighted. There was much to be done. David and Susie had big plans and together they enthused and energised everyone, not least of all each other. They had a few more months left of 1988 in which to get ready for yet another move — to bigger and better premises.

It was time, Susie decided, that she stopped cutting David's hair! She had done this for thirty years now, and she felt that the Governor Designate should have a professional barber. They tried it — once — and both agreed Susie's work was superior. David had very strong, wiry hair and rarely had to use a comb on it, instead he just pushed it into shape and there it stayed. It was the same in adulthood as in childhood when, at Scots College, he had always been the neatest of boys thanks to his fine head of hair.

The media decided it was time to find out more about the future Governor, arriving at his home very early one morning to be met by a knobbly-kneed, barefooted man in crumpled shorts. In the interviews that followed, the reporters realised he meant it when he said he had no time for 'sham, pretence or bullshit' and was not impressed by 'bludgers and whingers'. They discovered he was serious when he added that he loathed inefficiency and had no time for a show-off. They also learned that he was incredibly honest, very straight, down-to-earth, fun-loving, always enjoyed a good party and didn't suffer fools gladly. He admitted that when he was Captain he took up smoking a pipe until his officers said the sight made them nervous. He confessed that he liked feeling 'a bit anxious in the morning knowing there is something to be licked that day' and that he was going to miss Harry's Café de Wheels at Woolloomooloo, where he had often had a pie and peas with the sailors before they returned to their ships.

In answer to the question, 'Are you a traditionalist?', he replied, 'If you mean things like integrity, service and loyalty and all those sorts of things, yes, I am a traditionalist, but if you mean hanging on to minor trappings that don't matter, of course I am not'. He realised that the position was an honour bestowed on a privileged few, and recognised that the Governor symbolises the Constitution — indeed, is the custodian of the Constitution — and provides an apolitical voice in an otherwise political world.

The day the news broke, Susie was playing in the finals of the Bronze Championships at Royal Sydney Golf Club, which she won. She was therefore expected to stay at the Golf Club for the presentation and to make a speech. Asking if they could they delay the presentation for just a short time, she dashed home, did the required press interviews and returned to the club in time to receive the cup.

Australians soon learned that here was a couple who met commitments, genuinely cared and were not afraid to say so. There was no room for stuffiness in this position. After a lifetime of public service, David Martin was thoroughly groomed and geared for the role. The Martin style was honest, frank and open, and they took the office of Governor very seriously. They were going to open up Government House to the people — and everyone else concerned — and they were going to have fun along the way.

The Navy had paved the way for him. As he often quoted, 'The Navy discovered Australia, the Navy brought the first settlers to Australia, the Navy provided food and the first five Governors — Phillip, King, Bligh, Hunter and Macquarie— for Australia.'

CHAPTER NINE

FATHER OF THE YEAR

Keep your bat straight and run towards your catches

David was up a ladder putting together a bookcase in their home at Edgecliff, when the phone rang. 'Bloody phone', he muttered as he climbed down the ladder to answer it.

He returned a few minutes later, ascended the ladder once more and, whilst he busily went on with his work, he called over his shoulder to Susie in the sitting room, 'Remember I told you I was short-listed for Father of the Year? Well, they've just chosen me!'

'That's a great honour', said Susie.

'There must be someone more worthy.'

'It's very exciting', Susie persisted.

'I'm surprised people even know me!'

'You've become known through Tresco.'

'It must be because it's the Bicentennial year and I'm a double first fleeter.'

Always embarrassed by accolades, he was too modest to see that he was an obvious choice. Nevertheless, he admitted that he was 'thrilled' and, given that as the Commanding Officer of a ship at sea he had been known as Father, Dad and the Old Man, it had a good ring to it. He had taken to fatherhood like a duck to water and loved his three children dearly. Similarly, his five grandchildren were very important to him, too.

The Father of the Year, appointed by the Father's Day Council, must be well known in the community for his work in charity, the sciences or the military. He must be admired and respected by his contemporaries, peers and colleagues. The first Father of the Year in Australia in 1957 was Sir Edward Hallstrom. Others since include Sir Adrian Curlewis, Sir Roden Cutler, Sir Vincent Fairfax, Sir William McMahon, Major General Alan Stretton, Bobby Limb, Gary O'Callaghan, Professor Alfred Pollard. Quite an assembly.

Whilst his Naval career had prevented David from spending as much time at home with his family as he would have liked, when he was home, according to his children, things were 'extraordinarily good' — he was 'a terrific father', 'an excellent father', 'a fun father'. He was certainly the Father of the Year in their eyes.

David was approachable, had a great sense of fairness, was funny and very loving. A father who stood back till he was asked for advice rather than leaping in with it, believing 'when the pupil is ready, the teacher appears'. He was everything his children desired in a father. Hadn't he won the Fathers' Race at Kambala in 1972, beating Dr Edward Bates? And didn't every one of his letters, written from all over the world, offer fatherly help and support?

Darling Sandy,

Deciding about the next few years will be a bit difficult for you — just try to work out what you want to do (and *why*) then we will help you and fight for you and love you. I'm happy over here. I'd love you to see it all with me. Please be happy (won't it be good just to have your plate at night).

Darling Annapot,

Sorry about the question on my last page to Mum, but her writing is not too good. I hope you've gotten over it (now I always say 'gotten'). This place Carmel is just deevine. And expensive. They buy expensive antiques in England and re-sell them here for ten times as much. Be a little love and av fun.

Dear Billie Boy,

I was so pleased that you were asked to try with the rep team — good on you. As long as you always try your best and go for it hard I'll be pleased with you. And that goes for picking up dog pooh too! Most of the blokes on this course are dum dums.

His affectionate greetings to William ranged from 'Dear My Son', 'Dear My Boy Bill' and 'Dear Willie' to 'Dear Chess Champion, footy expert, dog pooh picker-up Willie'. The farewells were just as original: 'Have fun and go for that ball', 'Hooray for taking a wicket and catching a catch', 'I hope you're having a good time *and* cleaning your shoes', 'Keep your bat straight and run towards your catches', 'be good old son', and 'don't forget to tackle hard, slam the ball in, pick up the dog pooh and be a good prefect. And look after our women for me!'

After seeing the stirring movie *Gallipoli*, David was inspired by the dialogue between Jack and Archy:

What are your legs?
Springs. Steel springs.
What are they going to do?
Hurl me down the track.
How fast can you run?
As fast as a leopard.
How fast *are* you going to run?
As fast as a leopard
Then let's see you do it!

Years later, when playing rugby for his school and Navy Colts, William was urged by his father to 'run as fast as a leopard' and to 'tackle for the Lord', believing that any God-given gift should be put to use.

Sandy and Anna received equally loving cards, beginning with 'Darling Girls', 'Darling Annapot', 'Darling Sambo' and ending with, 'Good luck with your exams my sausage and have fun'.

In another postcard to the girls he wrote humorously, displaying his sense of the absurd:

> The Royal Yacht looks pretty good and we are steaming along half a mile from her, protecting her from flying fish, rain, flying saucers, rabbits on motorbikes, and all such things. So far we're winning, and she hasn't been attacked once!

Family discussions, on everything, were held regularly. The children would save up their joys, worries and stories, and as soon as David arrived home it would all come tumbling out. Because things at sea were strictly run, he bent over backwards to make sure this did not happen at home. Instead, anything of importance was discussed, thrashed out and agreed to by all. When he had received a posting to Sydney, they all had their say as to whether they should move house, yet again, and change schools. The upshot was, they didn't. Instead, for eighteen months, recognising the importance of his children remaining at good schools, David commuted from Canberra to Sydney — and enjoyed it!

Important news had to be told to the children, simultaneously if possible, so when David was offered the position of Governor of New South Wales, he ensured Anna and Will were home and, once he had Sandy on the phone in Nowra, he let them all know together. That way they were all put in the picture at the same time.

The Martins also had expressions peculiar to their family, which only they knew and used. One of these sayings dated back to David's teens, when he was staying with family friends, the Hawkes, on their property in South Australia. David and Bob Hawkes were out in the paddock and Bob accidentally shot himself in the foot with his rifle. David ran back to the homestead shouting to Mrs Hawkes, 'Toe toe toe! Bob has shot himself in the toe!' meaning, 'Don't worry too much, it's not desperate, he's fine, it could have been a lot worse'. On another occasion it was 'Toe toe toe! Sandy has written off the car', but the underlying message was 'Sandy is not hurt, it's only the car'. They found this to be a concise and practical way of conveying a message and no one misused the wording.

Sandy, Anna and Will felt they were never treated like children. Rather, they felt like grown-ups with their Dad. He never said 'you're too little' or 'you're not old enough'. He was young at heart himself. So long as everyone was trying their hardest, striving, it didn't matter if it didn't work if you'd given it your best. 'The joy of trying makes life worthwhile', he explained.

In addition to the family discussions, David knew the value of one-to-one 'chats' with his children. Whenever he could, he'd drive from Canberra to Sydney to visit his mother, taking only one child with him. Strapped in the car for three and a half hours each way, many a problem was solved. He loved to talk as well as listen. The only problem was that he found it difficult to concentrate on driving and talking simultaneously, so he just went faster at both. Once he was booked for speeding at Goulburn on the way up to Sydney and again at Goulburn on the way back. When Anna remarked, 'Dad, it would have been cheaper to fly', he merely said, 'Bloody hell, it would have been, too' and resumed the conversation — keeping a wary eye on the speedo!

When David returned from sea, he always arrived home bearing Smarties and, in turn, the children had them at the ready for him. It was a reciprocal ritual which they all enjoyed and it cost little. Money was always a bit of a problem, as it is in all Naval families.

On one occasion, he enthusiastically produced a watch he'd bought in Hong Kong for Will, but when he heard that Will had shoplifted a coffee crisp from the Minit Market in Fisher, ACT, he withdrew it until later on when it was deserved. Although Susie had already taken Will and his partner-in-crime to face the music and apologise to the shop owner, the watch was 'on hold' until merited.

To Will, the only son, childhood was growing up with Mum, and Dad at weekends. Whilst his father was away, Will would bring 'the women' cups of tea every morning, mow the lawn and pick up the inevitable dog droppings, but he ceased to do these things the minute his father returned. Once David had gone again, Will would resume those duties.

Sport was important to the Martins. Will loved golf, tennis and skiing. He recalls how his father would adopt a 'special concentrating expression' on his face during a game of golf when he'd dig up the turf, muttering to himself as he replaced it, 'Bloody stupid game anyway'. He was 'as stiff as a rod' at tennis, Will remembers. 'If he'd put all the effort into hitting the ball that he put into making the accompanying noises, he'd have been okay'. But, as it turned out, Will and Susie were better sporting partners and opponents. This was something David envied, though he was not jealous of the interaction. As a child, Will had been especially close to his mother, but once he joined the Navy, he and his father had so many common interests that their friendship grew and grew.

Maintaining the proud Martin tradition of seafaring, William is now a Lieutenant Commander in the Royal Australian Navy. He believes the Navy is a 'wonderful institution and, although changing very rapidly, represents splendid opportunities and offers great direction and stability'. He feels it is a worthwhile career for young men and women because teamwork, interacting with other people and working towards common goals are important. 'A couple of hundred people in a tin can at sea have to have a common aim. That's why we all work for "Father" — the ship is one man and we all support him. The ship has to have a good team or it all falls to pieces. Dad had a firm belief that there was no one in a ship who was more important than another. I think that's why the junior sailors respected him so much, because he respected them and acknowledged that the part played by *every* member of the team was vital. It only took one person to forget or neglect to turn on a fire fighting hose and the ship could be lost.' Like father, like son. Like Navy, like home.

Will has many anecdotes about his father, illustrating the respect with which he was regarded by sailors. Stories such as: 'You wouldn't believe it, one day I was down in the boiler room and had my head stuck in a boiler and I put my hand out for a spanner and I couldn't reach it. So I called out "Someone give me a bloody spanner" and this bloke in white overalls gave it to me — who was it but Father!'

David would often visit the junior sailors and it was no trouble for him to pass a spanner. He was naturally helpful and related well to people of all ages, seniority and background. He had no time for anyone 'swinging the lead'. He used to say, 'Your Navy is not just leadership and discipline, it must also be fun, and Navy life is'. He had begun as a good follower. Then as a good leader he had the ability to make everyone feel special. He wasn't just the Captain upstairs in the cushy chair, he was down there with the the sailors in the boiler room, too. He cared about everyone. He had great respect and regard for his country and Queen and all that this represented. His Navy was there for his Queen. This same love was ingrained in his family. After each loyal toast to 'the Queen', he would smile contentedly and add fervently, 'God bless her'.

This was the same man who gave Anna a bottle of Southern Comfort on her sixteenth birthday and, from time to time, urged her to drink it with him. He was horrified when she added Coca Cola to it. When the Martins held parties, Sandy, Anna and Will's friends usually gravitated to wherever David was rather than to their peers, such was his interest in them and theirs in him.

Sandy and her husband — Commander Vince Di Pietro, a Fleet Air Arm Pilot — are located at Australia House in London for three years, where he is Staff Officer Co-ordinating and she is the Community Liaison Officer. They have three daughters: Flavia, Louisa and Olivia.

Sandy sees the family as the absolute core of life and living in London means long absences from those she loves. She recalls:

> I grew up in the knowledge that I could approach my parents about anything. Dad encouraged us to share concerns, anxieties, happiness and discoveries with him at any time and, even as a troubled teenager, I always felt that no matter what the problem, I could talk to Dad about it. He was totally approachable and always listened. His answers were carefully thought out and reliable.
>
> We had wonderful bedtime rides to bed as little children which involved riding on Dad's back all the way to our room where, once deposited, Dad would turn around in order to retrieve the second and then third child for their turn. We'd never tire of the delight involved in making the choice. In fact, Dad was a young and very active father and didn't seem

to get impatient or tired of the games with his three young children. An image I have is of him sitting in the bathroom, still in his Naval uniform, playing his ukulele and singing 'Old Black Joe' (which was one of only two songs he could play on it) to us while we were in the bath. We'd ask him to sing it again and again, and I still can hear his gentle voice and slightly uneven strumming.

Dad, like Mum, never shouted or smacked. He did threaten to knock our blocks together occasionally and in fact once did. I think we were fighting incessantly in the back seat of the car at the time. Our parents were strict but fair. I'm sure this is what anyone who had ever worked for Dad would say. He expected high standards and was firm, decisive, always listened carefully and was always fair. The only people Dad didn't like were those who were dishonest, apathetic, lazy or who 'knocked' things unnecessarily. My six words to sum him up: Gentle. Dignified. Compassionate. Courageous. Honest. Humorous.

Anna's husband, Michael Beaumont, is an auctioneer and a musician. Anna's training and interests are based on food and catering. They have two sons, Thomas and Elliot, and live in Sydney. The 'old salts' tradition continues; it's in the blood, right through generations. Anna remembers:

Manners were important to Dad and we were schooled in them from an early age. He also took it upon himself to educate all our friends — a habit I've taken on with our two boys.

Our school friends were required to present themselves to say hello on arrival at our house for visits or parties and to say goodbye before they left.

My 'dates' and Sandy's were always asked in for a drink and a chat and invariably ended up spending time with Mum and Dad. Most grown-ups don't bother to talk with teenagers. Instead of making our friends feel small, it gave them confidence. Dad had a way of making people feel special, from small children through to the oldies, who especially loved him.

We were allowed enormous freedom compared to most of our friends, but that came as a result of the trust he placed in us. The family was all-important to us and we received such love, support and security that we never doubted we could do anything.

There were several things that my father taught me that have saved me often: never write anything down that might incriminate you, try not to lend money to friends and, his favourite, it's not how you get into trouble ... it's how you get out of it.

On the day of my wedding, he and I rode together to the church. He asked the driver to stop just at the top of the hill and turned to me and said, 'This is your last chance to change your mind if you want to. We'll just tell everyone we're having a party instead'! I assured him I was happy and we went on our merry way.

No family is complete without a dog. First there was Gobi, the colour of sand, appropriately named after the desert. When only six weeks old, Gobi looked more like a calf, weighing 'hundreds of pounds'. They had answered an advertisement, attracted by the description. When they saw him, they just had to adopt him.

Benji, by contrast, was a very small dog and was first seen at his birth by Sandy, who said, 'We'll just have *that* one'. Benji was much loved, intelligent and dignified. He was also a show-off! After performing his tricks, he would go up to each member of the family as if to enquire 'What did you think of that?'. Everyone would smile, clap and say, 'Do it again, Benji'. It was just like a circus act — he would run to the end of the room, make sure he had their full attention, then do it again, and again and again. His master thought of him as 'a cross between a flying fox and a cabanossi sausage'. He was so often photographed at Government House that one of the later pictures in the press was simply entitled 'Benji and the Governor'.

In his speech as Father of the Year, David stressed that the title, especially in these times of anti-discrimination, should have been given to Susie and his children. He saluted her for the job she had done as father as well as mother and thanked his family for coping with their nomadic parents. 'Because of us, the most that they had learned in their many schools was how to say goodbye to their friends.' He also made mention of two 'foster fathers' who had been so important in his life — Scots College, and teacher Robert Edyvene, who had died at the great age of ninety-seven.

There was no doubt in all of their minds (Benji's too!) that David Martin — Father, Dad, the Old Man, Skip or Captain, whatever the title — was the right choice for Father of the Year. Any year. And in his mind, one should 'never refuse; accept graciously'. He always considered himself to be lucky and privileged. He couldn't quite understand it, and was a little uncomfortable, when vast numbers of letters of congratulations arrived from Australians far and wide. 'Bloody hell, they don't even know me', was his response. He never fully understood how much his own influence and example affected others.

CHAPTER TEN

ENTER GOVERNMENT HOUSE

A sublime example of democracy at work

Sir David Martin entered Government House with a spring in his step, boundless energy and a passion for the post, believing he was there to serve the people of New South Wales. He made the transition with an easy grace. He was on the crest of a wave.

After leaving their house at Edgecliff and storing their furniture yet again, the Martins began their move to Government House by staying overnight in a suite at the Hotel Inter-Continental, Sydney. Here, on 20 January 1989, they prepared for the swearing-in ceremony. Susie spent a long time getting ready, dressing carefully, making sure that her hair was 'just right' before positioning her hat at the correct angle. Satisfied at last, she went in to see how David was progressing. She found him still in his pyjamas! Overeager, she was ready an hour too soon. Off came the hat and they relaxed together instead.

An hour later, when they arrived at Parliament House, the same hat was knocked off her head as she alighted from the car. Muttering something unprintable, Susie plonked it straight back where it belonged, making a mental note to watch her language!

Sir David Martin became the thirty-fourth Governor of the State of New South Wales, succeeding Sir James Rowland. In his swearing-in speech he announced: 'My wife and I are committed to helping those who help others'. This became his mission.

Once outside, Sir David inspected the Guard of Honour, then the Mounted Police Troop escorted the Rolls Royce, driven by the chauffeur Don Armitstead, to Government House. There, members of Susie's family from Victoria awaited them and were given a tour around the House. Today Government House is a far cry from the portable canvas and timber structure that Captain Arthur Phillip, the first Governor of New South Wales, had brought with him from England in 1788. Governor Lachlan Macquarie had declared in 1809, 'One day, a great city will be built on the shore of Sydney'. His words had come true. New South Wales, birthplace of modern Australia, governed by a Parliament elected by the people, covers more than 800 000 square kilometres, and Sydney, the State's capital and commercial centre, is acknowledged as the gateway to Australia.

Government House didn't seem the least bit strange to the Martins. They had visited this splendid sandstone edifice many times before and Susie Martin's mother, born Sylvia Knox Knight, is a great-great-niece of Sir George Gipps, who was the first inhabitant of the present Government House in Sydney.

Having lived in so many places, including Adelaide, London, Portsmouth, Malta, Jervis Bay, Canberra and Sydney, they were looking forward to a term of four years at Government House. David was fifty-six, so this would mean retirement at sixty. Ideal.

Prior to the swearing-in ceremony, Sir David met his Aide-de-Camp in Waiting, Lieutenant Colin Bold RANR, who had prepared a summary of the day's activities and instructed him in protocol. It is a quick learning process for both Governor and his aide. Adjustments to the other's needs have to be recognised and acted upon straight away. David was a little apprehensive about his swearing-in speech. He always put 100 per cent of himself into everything he did. The delivery was perfect — warm, relaxed and genuine — but in order to be that way, a great deal of time had to be spent on preparation so that it was 'spot on' and 'absolutely right'. He had many questions for Colin Bold: What will happen? What are their names? What is the age group? What are their interests?

David liked as much information as he could obtain before any function so he could project himself at the right level and leave the audience with an uplifting message. Using adjectives widely, his words became pictures. His speeches were succinct, straight to the point. He never preached, he was frank, fair, and often blunt, urging all Australians to 'stop whingeing and get on with the future'. Every speech was tailor-made for the occasion, with symbols and slogans and always a message to take away. Whether the audience was small or large, critical or supportive, seven years old or seventy, there was something of worth for them all. He had a personal story for every subject. When talking to judges on the importance of their decision-making powers, he would point out that, in his many years at sea, the ship's Captain was also the ship's judge — and jury! He saw every speech as an opportunity to spread the word about the Vice-Regal role.

His love of speech-making could be traced back many years to his very early days at Scots College. He had made scores of speeches on a great variety of topics and all had been acknowledged as splendid. When his childhood friend Bill Hunter was married in 1971, David proposed the toast to the bride and groom. He had spent all morning walking round the Botanic Gardens in Brisbane thinking about what he was going to say, polishing the speech and brushing it up. It was worth the homework. Many of the guests still talk about it!

As Colin Bold recalls: 'He inspired everyone around him to achieve their best. I remember one day I was playing tennis at Government House and I was losing badly when Sir David, taking a stroll, paused to watch. Immediately I put 200 per cent of myself into the game and ended up with a convincing victory. I felt I had to perform better, to do my very best for his sake.'

One of the first things Sir David did once ensconced at Government House was to arrange for a video to be made. Written, edited, produced and directed by film-maker Reg Robertson and sponsored by the State Bank of New South Wales as a community service, it was distributed to every secondary school in the State. It concerned David that many people did not fully realise what the Governor's role was and rarely recognised the face of the Queen's representative. He also invited two senior students from various secondary schools throughout New South Wales to Government House to see the Governor face-to-face, to learn first-hand more about the Office and to understand the gubernatorial position. He considered that only by knowing the facts could the people judge for themselves the benefits derived from having a Governor — a Governor who represents the Queen and the people of New South Wales, a role which he described as 'a sublime example of democracy at work'.

He advised the students that there are three dominant facets — three Capital Cs — to the role of Governor: Constitutional, Ceremonial and Community. All three are subtly interwoven; each supports the other. The most important of these, Constitutional, is the reason there is a Governor. It is the hinge on which everything swings.

The Governor presides over the Executive Council, comprised of Ministers of State. He approves and signs documents, Bills, Proclamations, Orders, Council minutes and many other items which are dealt with by the Council. The Governor's approval is not automatic. Whilst he does not have the power to make amendments, he can refer a matter back to the Minister or Head of Department if he is concerned. This important function ensures that matters which have been proposed, even if they have Cabinet or a Minister's approval, are scrutinised so that they do not unwittingly affect other parts of government. The Governor, in giving Royal Assent by signing a Bill, is recognising the authority of Parliament and representing the interests of the people. The students learned that a Bill that has been through Parliament cannot be made law, nor can an important appointment be made, unless it has Royal Assent.

The Governor appoints and dismisses Ministers on the advice of the Premier. The Governor is required to take the advice of his Ministers as long as they represent the majority, democratically elected government. He stressed that if a political party cannot form a government or is still in office when it has lost its majority, then the Governor of the day has 'Reserve Power'. Further, the Governor is not responsible to the Governor-General. There is no chain of command from a State Governor to the Governor-General. Nor is there any link between the Governor and the British government or any member of the British government. The Governor has a link to the Queen of Australia, whom he represents — not to the British government.

The Governor cannot vote, nor does he pay taxes. In response to the question 'How much power do you have?', Sir David replied that he had almost none at all. He then put the question another way. It was important, he said, to ask 'How much power does the Governor's presence deny to ministers who would otherwise have absolute power?'.

The second C, Ceremonial, is succinct. David quickly observed that Australians love a good ceremony, with real meaning, but not too much of it. So short and stylish it became. As the Queen's representative, it is the Governor's responsibility to open Parliament and swear in Ministers and Supreme Court Judges. There are many major award ceremonies, a multitude of functions to attend, reception of visiting dignitaries, and the Governor either visits or entertains more than fifty charitable organisations a year.

The third C, Community, is far-reaching, and includes visiting people in hospitals, factories, gaols, sheltered workshops, rubbish-recycling plants, nurseries, mental homes, schools, emergency services, welfare institutions, service organisations, clubs, rehabilitation centres, homes for the elderly. An enormous cross-section was involved in Sir David's plan to 'meet a group of people we haven't met before'. This is a vital part of the Governor's role, for a Governor who regularly makes country visits, meets hospital staff, visits sheltered workshops and talks with and listens to everyday Australians in his Community role takes this broader knowledge back to the Executive Council in his Constitutional role. Drawing on Walter Bagehot's celebrated book on the English constitution, David referred to the three rights of a Constitutional Monarch: 'the right to be consulted, the right to encourage, the right to warn'. He believed these rights became responsibilities — to be informed, to encourage, to warn.

Through this 'meet the people' philosophy and service to others, Sir David and Lady Martin brought personal sincerity and warmth to thousands. It was a seven day a week commitment. The hours of duty were elastic, often from eight-thirty in the morning until ten-thirty at night with several functions in between — and, of course, the Dawn Service on Anzac Day meant a very early start to the day's activities. The importance of these Vice-Regal visits allowed the dedicated staff in the organisations involved to know that their work was recognised and appreciated, and focused the attention of the public and various authorities on many social problems which otherwise may have remained unnoticed.

Before moving to Government House, David talked to friends about 'playing the role' there. The sister of his old friend George Halley reminded him 'the role is already there — you only have to be it'. The Office of Governor is more important than the person.

David had a great belief in the position of Governor, recognising that not only must the dignity of the Office be upheld, but that it was also important that he relate to people at all levels. He possessed that rare gift of maintaining a fine balance between the two. He was very keen to adhere to correct protocol and procedure but at the same time wanted everyone to feel welcome and comfortable. Every occasion must be proper and dignified as well as friendly and fun, and under no circumstances was it to be stuffy.

He was not a perfectionist or obsessive, but he attended to every detail, always striving to get it right and to do it correctly. He once said, 'The importance of protocol is the standardisation of putting people at ease so that you can then get on with what *is* important'. Nor did he regard protocol as a closed book; instead, it represented excellent guidelines.

So, having established that, he made sure that all the organisers and hosts of functions which he would attend were alerted to the ceremonial duties of sitting and standing at the right time; the first form of address was 'Your Excellency' then 'Sir' thereafter, and he specified that the Vice-Regal 'top' table be replaced with a round one so that everyone could participate. A round table was more sociable; he wanted every person to speak and to listen to his hosts and guests alike. As David wore a hearing aid, it was important that he was seated close to his guests rather than in one long, straight line. He disliked the expression 'please be upstanding', explaining that people weren't invited to 'be downsitting', but he failed to eliminate it.

The invitations poured in. He considered them all carefully. It was impossible to attend everything, therefore he selected those in line with his overriding purpose of 'helping those who help others'. So it was those with special needs, the disabled, the speech days at schools where a Governor had never attended previously, state schools as well as private schools, who benefited from his smiling presence.

Every Wednesday morning there was a 'round table' conference attended by Sir David, Colin Bold, his personal private secretary Captain J.O. (Jo) Morrice RAN (retired), the Official Secretary Alan McKenzie, Lady Martin and her personal secretary Sarah Adams ... and Benji. Here, in a frank and open style, they discussed and planned activities with diaries poised.

Sarah Adams's father, Commodore Harold Adams RAN (retired), had been in the Naval intake just before David, and she had known 'Davo and Susie' all her life. When she heard David being interviewed on radio prior to his coming to Government House, she immediately contacted him and asked could she have a chat and be considered for a position. They talked, she officially applied for a job and became Susie's personal secretary.

'I made an intellectual and emotional commitment for two years', says Sarah. 'My father described that time as "Camelot" and in many ways it was. The great trick was to keep everything in perspective, moving out of the real world and into fantasy land. We worked very hard but there was magic in it. The magic of working for Sir David. We were a team and a lot of what we did was inspirational.'

Colin Bold feels the same way. Loyal and dutiful, he made sure that precision and synchronisation were added to the enthusiasm, excitement and variety of ideas which already existed. He would often visit the location of an event, pacing it out carefully — sometimes several times — before he was completely satisfied. After each function he would be absolutely exhausted, often sad when it was over, but mostly on a high at its success. He, too, loved being a part of it all. He was constantly asked by function organisers if there were any strict dietary requirements for Sir David. His answer was always the same — 'No wobbly desserts, please'. David's large appetite and enjoyment of food embraced just about everything, except desserts that 'wobbled'.

Flummery and jelly were out and crème caramel was unthinkable.

Jo Morrice came to the position in April 1989, bringing with him a gift for detail. Every 'i' was dotted, every 't' was crossed, and capital letters were used for emphasis! He was dedicated and spent time and effort thinking about what was genuinely best for the Office. He had followed David through the Royal Australian Navy College and although they never actually served together, being of similar vintage, they were always good friends. Jo recalls:

> On assuming the position of Private Secretary, I quickly learnt that Sir David was not a man to beat about the bush. He was direct and at times unforgiving, but he valued advice and often sought opinions from members of his personal staff. I admired him for his fortitude and I shared his high ideals, especially his desire to uphold the dignity, traditions and authority of the Office of Governor. The path we trod together was not all smooth going — indeed, at times it was rocky — nevertheless I found the experience of working with David to be immensely challenging and, more often than not, rewarding. As a Governor, Sir David Martin was an exceptional leader, and he drew much admiration from all parts of society. He was quick to give credit where it was due, and his recognition and support for his personal and household staff was never lacking. It was damn hard work being the thirty-fourth Governor's Private Secretary, but I dare say Sir David would have agreed that it was hard work being a damn good Governor, which he undoubtedly was.

Benji settled into his new role as watchdog at Government House very quickly. He loved having his own ID card, the House suited him, his meals were good and there were cameras everywhere! He wagged his tail so often that Sarah remarked, 'Benji has a great smile but his tail is too big for him'. He was a splendid ice-breaker when visitors arrived — he'd slip in with their legs and behind their clothes — but he knew the rules. He was not allowed in the dining room at Government House and he never once disobeyed. As the dining room adjoined another reception room, with a differently patterned carpet, Benji would sit with his nose *on* the line between the two, never over it.

Colin Bold was working late one night at Government House and when he went outside for a moment, he saw that Benji had left a 'little message' on the carpet. Colin thought, 'I can't face this at the moment — the footman will see it and fix it', and he went back to his work. A little later, he heard a sound and went outside again. There was David cleaning it up.

'Sir, you can't do that — let me.'

'No, I always clean up after my dog', said David.

Likewise after barbecues or outdoor entertaining, Susie would do the same thing. They were both very down-to-earth.

Always aware that he was the Queen's representative, Sir David would ask himself, 'Would the Queen do this?' and if he felt that his Sovereign would not open a controversial exhibition or hotel or attend a questionable occasion, then he wouldn't either. He could be quite blunt and quick to point out if others didn't measure up to his expectations. On a visit to the country, he said to some men in the crowd, 'I noticed you didn't take off your hats when the anthem was played today. I expect *you* to set an example'. He said similar things to parliamentarians and other leaders, too.

'He's no pushover — you just can't pass a Bill' was overheard at Government House. On another occasion he was talking to students who, in the future, would represent Australia overseas. He asked one foreign affairs exchange student what his aspirations were. His response was terse: 'Standing around making small talk like this isn't really my idea of what the job should entail'. David dismissed him with, 'Stand up straight, take your hands out of your pockets and you may now go'. The student departed, his arms swinging!

David wanted everyone to do his or her best; he wanted excellence. 'Excellence has no horizons', he told students at Narooma when they celebrated their school centenary. 'The great thing about excellence is it's always there, you can always go for it and there's always a bit more to get if you keep trying.'

He encouraged all Australians to 'honour our country, our flag and our Sovereign'. Always a leader, he now became a great leader. 'There is nothing we can't handle if we've got faith in it', he'd urge.

'Sing up, Colin', he'd mouth to his aide if he felt the anthem lacked the required vocal gusto. Again, just as in the game of tennis, Colin put in 200 per cent! On another occasion he said to Sarah, 'I don't think you gave of your best today, I think you'll find …'. The criticism was always constructive. 'He'd make you reflect, then he'd smile and you'd smile back and you'd think, "I can improve, he's actually doing me a favour" — and he was', Sarah recalls. David didn't see himself as merely a figurehead, he was there to solve problems too.

Every day brought new thoughts, new ideas. He was constantly thinking about how procedures could be improved and urging everyone to look at things in a new way. It was refreshing to see how even simple little problems could be solved if different methods were used. Were some traditions worth questioning? Were they useless? Worth maintaining? Could they be improved? He made constant notes on little pieces of paper and Sarah would give him words and pictures, providing substantial input for his speeches. It was a happy working environment, a very natural one. As natural as the man himself and his idiosyncracies, such as keeping liquorice allsorts in his top drawer!

Whilst David went at a great pace almost every minute of every day, he was very keen for others to relax and enjoy themselves, and would often say to Colin, 'Go out and have a really good time. Just make sure you take a self-addressed envelope and mail yourself back to me in the morning.'

David never forgot his old school. As Governor, he opened Glengarry. Conducted by Scots College, it is an Outward Bound-type school on 400 hectares at Kangaroo Valley, New South Wales, where Year 9 students spend six months of the year. Orienteering, rock climbing, bush crafts and abseiling preoccupy them. There is a cattle stud, no television and no telephones. It is a wonderful enterprise and a great success. David always held Scots College in high esteem. In any written correspond-ence with the College, he would always sign off with 'STTF', meaning 'Scots to the fore'. At a dinner given in his honour at The School's Club by his old friends, he spoke of his admiration and appreciation of the College, saying that Scots had never sent an account to the Martins. 'We couldn't have paid it anyway', he added. He then went round the room and said a few words about every single person present. On another occasion, he attended a farewell dinner for a schoolmaster from Scots at the University of Sydney. He did not attend in an official capacity, but as a former, appreciative pupil — he was just 'one of the boys'.

The year 1989 was a fruitful, stimulating, busy year. In addition to his philosophy of 'helping those who help others', there were 'bring the children into Government House', 'take the Governor to meet the people' and 'learn how the system works'. He became very interested in a number of government organisations and asked Alan McKenzie to contact the people who did the work. The Fire Brigade, the 'waste paper people', the Police, the Ambulance Service and similar bodies all received a visit. Behind the scenes, they referred to such occasions as 'the recycling lunch', 'the road carnage lunch', 'the waifs and strays lunch', 'the business and union leaders lunch' and so on. His legendary sense of humour never deserted him, and returning from the sewerage works at North Head, where he had become an expert on effluent, he smiled at his Aide-de-Camp and said, 'When you get home, Colin, I'd like you to wash your hair — not once, not twice, but three times please!'.

Susie's schedule was equally demanding — often three or four major events in a day. What she really missed at Government House was doing some cooking, which she had always enjoyed. Ralph, the chef, had worked for five Governors, so he was very accustomed to doing things his way. Consequently, when their grandchildren came to 'Gumnut House', as they called it, there was very little that was suitable for them to eat. In time, things altered.

When the opportunity presented itself, David and Susie would have a private drink together upstairs before coming down to dinner. Early in his Governorship, a maid came to turn down the bed and literally bumped into David, stark naked, coming back from a shower. They both apologised; he for not wearing a gown, she for coming upstairs too soon.

A few evenings later, Susie discovered a member of staff peering through a peephole, near the pantry. Surprised, she enquired why and was told, 'We're not to go upstairs until we see the Governor actually sitting down to dinner'.

Following the precedent established by Sir James Rowland, Sir David and Lady Martin often travelled long distances to country areas. Everyone seemed to respond to their warmth and friendliness and wanted to please. After a visit to a retirement home which left him a little depressed, David said seriously to Susie, 'You must promise me two things. One, never buy me a tracksuit; and two, never let me push the trolley behind you at supermarkets.' Susie nodded in agreement.

These visits to distant country towns were organised carefully. For many country people it was a red letter day. They had never received a Governor before. Sir David's appointment book records visits to places as far-flung as Barmedman, Gidginbung. He learned afterwards that the sale of paint had soared in each of the townships he visited, as everyone spruced up their houses for the once-in-a-lifetime experience.

On one particularly long country visit, which included visiting three locations in one stopover, with four or five functions each day, the whole party had been thoroughly wined and dined. The customary country hospitality coupled with extremely generous helpings and several courses on each occasion had meant non-stop eating. On the journey home, exhausted, they sank into the train's comfortable carriage, preparing to loosen their belts and relax.

The Chief of Railways had other ideas. Wanting to do the very best for the Governor and his party, railway staff had prepared a sumptuous banquet. In it came, a proper elegant full silver service, four knives one side, four forks the other, the best wines, lobster, course after course, finishing with … crème caramel!

They all exchanged glances. David warned that under no circumstances could they offend the railways who had catered so generously, and urged everyone to 'eat up'. When the staff came to clear away, all the food had gone. Rumour has it that no one had any breakfast the following morning and, thanks to the bread rolls that were tossed out the window, the wildlife flourished.

A few months later, at a leading venue in a city hotel where David was guest of honour, Colin Bold glanced at the printed menu. Sure enough, crème caramel. Quietly, he had a word with the organiser and by the time dessert arrived there were hundreds of little wobbly custards and one plate of fresh fruit. On the way home, David remarked, 'I knew you had your hand in that one, Colin'.

David was accustomed to answering questions from children and he actively encouraged them. There was no restraint. 'How old are you?' received the reply, 'How old are *you*?'. The child answered 'Six'. David responded with a smile, 'I was six once but last time I looked I was fifty-six'. To 'Do you ever get into trouble?', the Governor replied, 'We all try very hard around here, so no, we don't really get into trouble, we just do our best'.

'What's a Navy?', 'Where did you get your wife?', 'How did you fall in love?', 'Why do you travel in the back of the car — won't your Mum let you sit in the front?', 'How much is this house worth?', 'Have you ever been broken into?' David always answered children's questions to their satisfaction and he sent them off with a reminder to be 'fair dinkum'. He especially valued the remark of one child who told him solemnly, 'You've burnt yourselves into my memory'.

Always a friend to the young and disadvantaged, Sir David and Lady Martin held a Christmas party on 1 December at Government House. A little girl asked him, 'May I have the loudspeaker please? It has such lovely voices in it.' That same afternoon, Susie saw her husband holding, very carefully, an icecream in a cone. The child had said, 'Hey, Mister, would you please hold this while I go to the toilet?'. The little boy didn't come back, but David stood there for quite a while, such was his devotion to duty. Not wishing to disappoint a child, he explained, 'Just in case he does come back, I must wait here'.

Prior to the Christmas party, David went to Grace Bros city store to buy a Father Christmas hat. When he enquired where he'd find such an item, he was told 'two floors up'. On the first floor he was met by a representative of the store who hospitably accompanied him to where the hats were displayed. The system was working: the people of

New South Wales were recognising their Governor. In truth, he was a little disappointed, because he'd intended having some fun trying on a variety of Santa hats on his own. He had always loved and possessed a variety of hats — which was just as well, because as Governor he wore many. He was Chief Scout, Honorary Colonel of the Royal New South Wales Regiment and Honorary Commodore of No. 22 Squadron RAAF. The Fire Brigade had given him a helmet, there was one from the Boys' Brigade, the Jewish fraternity had honoured him too, as well as VicRail. There was his hat for the races and, a great favourite, a cotton cap embroidered by Sandy with the words 'Brave Dave'.

Nineteen eighty-nine passed in a flash. At Christmas time they went to Jervis Bay and, very soon afterwards, to Newcastle, where they comforted the earthquake victims. Noel Dodwell, the pilot from the State Roads and Traffic Authority, got them there in 40 minutes in a helicopter which took off from the front lawn of Government House.

Early in 1990, a few tell-tale signs of David's deteriorating health began to emerge. He did not feel well, did not want to eat and, for the first time, he had to cancel a trip to Coonabarabran, which Susie took in his stead. On another occasion he was forced to leave a reception early in Wagga Wagga. He may have had his suspicions that his malaise was a creeping thing, that there was more to it than met the eye, but he never gave any indication. He became grey, breathless and tired. 'Is he well?' his family and staff were constantly asked. 'He's perfectly alright', they replied, because what he was doing was so important. They were all tired. Why put a spanner in the works? They were doing good things. They must all keep going.

In May 1990, David was diagnosed as having mesothelioma. A fatal, virulent cancer. Death by suffocation. As the tumour was on the lining of the lungs, it was unable to be treated or removed. His voice came in spurts.

He called in members of staff one by one. They learnt that he must resign his post and 'fight this thing'. Susie, as ever, was at his side. Jo Morrice read out what David had written to all members of staff in order to save his breath.

The people of New South Wales were shocked when they heard

the news the following day. Nick Greiner broke down and wept as he told Members of Parliament about the illness and that Sir David Martin would be retiring as early as August. David wrote to the Queen on 25 May 1990 to inform her of his retirement.

> Your Majesty,
>
> I must relinquish my Commission as the Governor of New South Wales. This decision has been made with deep sadness, and I regret having to inform you of it.
>
> My wife and I would like you to know that the job of representing Your Majesty has been a great privilege and a wonderful experience. We have been very happy indeed in our busy and exciting life of Vice-Regal activities. It has been extremely rewarding.
>
> I am aware that you have already accepted my request for early retirement. Thank you.

He did not go out; instead, he delved into asbestos-related situations which he wanted made public. He now had time to do this. Sitting in his office, he still imposed this discipline on himself. He unearthed a great deal of information, some of it dating right back to the early 1940s. He discovered that his deadliest enemies had been the microfine asbestos fibres which lined various parts of ships. Asbestos was sprayed extensively for insulation and swaddling.

'The X-ray units would have been inundated with Service personnel', said Leo Duffy when he heard. 'He was the first in our era. Previously it couldn't be proved. All of us shipmates were devastated when we heard about Sir David. In *Melbourne*, the asbestos-related powder would fall down in your food or soup when planes would land on the flight deck just above.'

The deterioration in David's health was rapid. He suspected his time was running out. He felt robbed of opportunities. He knew what 'brave' meant — take the ship home or sink with it. He sometimes felt the vulnerability of humankind. Although he behaved bravely, he felt

GOVERNMENT HOUSE
SYDNEY 2000

25th May 1990

Your Majesty,

I must relinquish my Commission as the Governor of New South Wales. This decision has been made with deep sadness, and I regret having to inform you of it.

My wife and I would like you to know that the job of representing Your Majesty has been a great privilege and a wonderful experience. We have been very happy indeed in our busy and exciting life of Vice Regal activities. It has been extremely rewarding.

I am aware that you have already accepted my request for early retirement. Thank you.

Yours sincerely,
David Martin.

frail underneath. Everyone at Government House recognised the fire in him and tried to match it. No one there wanted to disappoint him.

Plastic tubing attached to his nostrils carried oxygen to assist his breathing. A spare oxygen bottle was ordered. As one ran out, the suppliers would deliver another.

During this difficult time, Susie's strength and support were unwavering. Colin Bold, observing the situation, phoned all church leaders asking for prayers for Sir David and the Martin family. The Cardinal, the Archbishop, Moderators and the Chief Rabbi, religious leaders of all faiths, responded in unity.

The new Governor Designate was Rear Admiral Peter Sinclair. Like Sir David, he had a distinguished Naval background. He, too, was a leader, and a man who found hard work no burden. He had been outstanding during the Nyngan floods in 1990 when he had been recalled from retirement to save the residents of the threatened country town. He would follow Sir David Martin and serve the people of New South Wales well. It was the passing of command between two Navy men. A case of a sailor taking the helm from his mate. As he said later, 'The Ship of State must remain on course' and he promised to maintain the course already established by the Martins.

Prior to Sir David, Air Marshal Sir James Rowland, a distinguished airman in World War II, had governed New South Wales. A Pathfinder pilot in Bomber Command, he had been a prisoner of war in Germany. He was the first engineer in RAAF history to become Chief of Air Staff. Lady Rowland had assisted in the restoration of Government House, and during their double term of eight years, they had set the mood for a friendly house. Prior to the Rowlands, Sir Roden Cutler, the thirty-second Governor, had resided at Government House for sixteen years (four terms) — Australia's longest-serving Governor. He was awarded the Victoria Cross for exceptional courage during World War II. All these Governors were great men and strongly complemented each other. Their wives, too, were exemplary. But of all the fine Governors, it was the spirited Sir Phillip Game whom David respected most and had hoped to emulate. Appointed in 1930 at the height of the Great Depression, Sir Phillip returned a quarter of his salary, and was the Governor who dismissed Premier Jack Lang and his

Cabinet because the Premier refused to pay State revenue to the Commonwealth.

Sir James Rowland had written a cheery little note to David on 19 January 1989, welcoming him as his successor and advising him, 'It's all yours'.

> Dear David
>
> A quick note to wish you both every success, which I am sure will be yours, and good health and every happiness here. The House itself is in pretty good shape; though Michel has a good deal of training to do with new staff, he is very good and engenders excellent atmosphere with your guests, which helps a lot. John H and Alan have my phone numbers if there is anything I can do to help at any time.
>
> Our warmest regards to you both — it's all yours.

David, in turn, compiled a guide which he passed on to Peter Sinclair. Headed 'My Child's Guide (a random collection of things I say to myself)', it comprised guidelines of dos and don'ts for the role of Governor.

> - You can't really leap into the 'warm and friendly' mode until you have established the dignity and stature. You may sometimes need to be very firm to preserve 'flags close-up', drum roll at the Opera House (the audience really likes it), the National Anthem played, and preferably sung, on your arrival at a function — (or the Vice-Regal salute if it's very pukka).
> - I am not important — the Office of Governor is.
> - People in Government House don't 'work for the Governor' — we all work together for the 'Office of Governor'.
> - The Governor represents the Queen of Australia — he doesn't report to her or work for her. As the Queen represents her people throughout the Commonwealth, therefore the Governor represents the people of New South

Wales. (I believe this fervently and I found that people want to hear it. If the Governor is to represent them, then he must know what they think, know how they feel and what they need. Thus, lots of meeting and listening).
- If you called somebody Sir before you were Governor, then continue to do so.
- Encourage and teach people to address you properly at all times, i.e. 'Your Excellency' (occasionally), 'Sir' (it's the most proper, but some people don't like doing it), 'Governor' (that is the best).
- Remember that those people you are about to meet today could look upon our meeting, or their visit to Government House, or this Investiture, as the biggest event in their lives. For you it's 'posing for yet another bloody photograph' but for them it's the picture of a lifetime. Do your best to make the moment enchanting for them.
- The Executive Council — rather the conversation afterwards — can be a very special occasion as the Governor's study is the only place in the world where Ministers can talk freely. Encourage them to talk. Remind them from time to time that this room is as secret as the confessional.
- The Prayer Breakfast was a great success. I do hope you will do it again in years to come.

Sadly, Sir David Martin's plans for the people of New South Wales, his family and his friends, were now thwarted. Time had come to leave Government House.

CHAPTER ELEVEN

EXIT GOVERNMENT HOUSE

All of us should stand up for what we believe in and should influence others to do the same

Sir David Martin exited Government House with the admiration and respect of everyone. In just a year and a half he had brought about many innovations and achieved much. He was ill, thin and very breathless.

Tuesday, 7 August 1990 duly arrived. A formal statement had been issued to the media and they came mid-morning in their numbers to Government House to hear his farewell speech. They hung on his every syllable. There were three dominant sounds in the room: the clicking of cameras, David's voice, and his laboured breathing. Ramrod straight, he told them how 'bitterly disappointed' he and Susie were at having to leave Government House early. They would have liked to have been more useful to the people of New South Wales.

Emotionally, he urged: 'All of us should stand up for what we believe in and should influence others to do the same. And what should we believe in? Well, just an Australian community which is fair, healthy, happy, industrious. Where children can grow up in safety, with hope and opportunity ... and fun.' He questioned, 'That's not too much to ask, is it?'. To their silent acquiescence he added, 'Well, let's go out and get it'.

He got through his speech without the use of oxygen. Earlier that same morning, there had been a rehearsal. In full regalia, and depending heavily on the oxygen, he delivered the speech which he had written with great care. His family attended the rehearsal. Susie never very far away, Sandy quietly watching, Anna soothing Elliot in the corner, Vince holding Olivia and Will listening intently. Satisfied with his striving and in the knowledge that he had done his best, David left the room. Benji followed faithfully. It was a very natural scene, with Benji providing a link between formality and friendliness.

Those with a keen eye for detail would have noticed that certain aspects of Sir David's uniform that day were not strictly correct. His son William and son-in-law Vince were helping him to dress and, as they donned his jacket, he told them to leave the aigulette over the sleeve and not pass the sleeve though it, as it was causing him some discomfort. He was also wearing the Order of Australia close to his neck, not, as correct procedure dictates, the KCMG with the AO beneath it. As they helped him put on his decorations, Vince was about to fasten the KCMG around his neck. 'Don't put that on because then you can't see the Order of Australia', said David. He wore the KCMG chest decoration on his left breast but wished to have the AO prominent and visible around his neck. Such was his loyalty to and love of Australia.

Then came presents for every single member of staff, all chosen by Susie. There were approximately fifty of them, including the cooks, the footmen, the butler, the housemaids, the cleaners, the kitchen hands, the front-of-house staff, the secretaries, the chauffeur, the housekeeper, the gatekeeper. No one had been forgotten. They were 'all champions'.

As the staff left, delighted with their treasured gifts, the Premier, Nick Greiner, arrived at 11.40 am. In answer to his question of 'How are you?', David replied, openly as ever, 'Quite apprehensive and quite out of breath'. They sat together while the Governor of New South Wales on his last day in office tried, literally, to gather his breath. Exhaling was impossible. When one is fighting for oxygen, one is concentrating totally on staying alive. As Jo Morrice put it, 'even thinking is taxing'.

The schedule was tight. At 11.56 am, Rear Admiral Horton (the Naval Support Commander) arrived at Government House and was given a general salute by the Service Guard of Honour. The Premier, now accompanied by his wife Kathryn, arrived at the parade and met, at precisely 12 pm, Sir David and Lady Martin. Rear Admiral Horton accompanied David to the saluting point, the Royal Salute by the Guard was given, then the official car moved into position in front of the saluting point, at the ready for departure. Only the very observant would have realised that Don, the thoughtful chauffeur, had parked right on the outside kerb. To save even one step for David was worthwhile.

As the car drove away, the nineteen-gun artillery salute commenced and Sir David gave the three-finger Scout salute to those who lined the way. Escorted by the Mounted Police Troop and preceded by motor cycle escort, the car advanced to Queen's Square. At the intersection of St James' Road and Macquarie Street, mounted police formed the Guard of Honour. The motor cycle escort proceeded with the car but broke off prior to its arrival at the new Martin house at Darley Road, Randwick. All this had occurred in twenty very short minutes. Inside the official car were the oxygen tubes and bottle. David declined to use them because he wanted things to appear as normal as possible. However, his instruction to Colin Bold was, 'but be ready'. In the car directly behind was Dr Michael Burns from St Vincent's Private Hospital — a regular and constant visitor to Government House over the past few months. He, too, was ready.

At the Sydney Football Stadium they transferred to Susie's little red car, BUN 200, before arriving at their new home, where packing cases greeted them and a million things were waiting to be unpacked. The move had been so rushed that by the time they moved into their new house, they were 'illegal' by a few hours because they still hadn't legally settled.

Sylvia Millear, Susie's mother, had always been a tower of strength. Never more so than when she first learned of her son-in-law's illness. She had come to stay at Government House, had kept the household calm and organised, and had provided stability and serenity. She was immensely respected by all who knew her.

Susie had continued attending all her official engagements as well as those she could manage of David's. She also attended to the packing, as well as looking for a new home for them. It hadn't been easy — there were four strict requirements. It must be readily available and affordable. It must be in working order, with nothing to be done and, most importantly, there must be no steps.

Throughout the generations, the women in the family had possessed great strength. First Esther Abrahams, strong-willed till the end. Jim Martin, too, had shown enormous strength of character. Now Susie Martin continued the tradition. She had been strong as a Naval wife, strong in support and was now particularly strong in adversity. All four of them — Esther, Jim, Sylvia and Susie — were stoics. All had confidence, self-esteem and were self-controlled. As well as being practical and down-to-earth, they were inspirational to others.

Just a couple of hours after arriving at their new home, David was admitted to St Vincent's Private Hospital. He was given a small room, no longer the large one he had previously occupied as Governor of New South Wales.

It had been a long and exhausting day. In answer to a nurse's enquiry of 'Have you got your own teeth?' he replied testily, 'Well, no one else's would fit me, would they?'. It was out of character for David to be anything other than courteous, but he was upset at being in hospital — all he wanted, right to the end, was to be at home with Susie. In an aside, the doctor said to her, 'Things aren't really good. I think it's weeks rather than months.'

With those less than heartening words ringing in her ears, Susie returned to Randwick to spend the first night in their new home. If the day had been a long and exhausting one for David, it had been no less taxing for Susie. It now seemed certain that the asbestos-related cancer, which had taken twenty to thirty years to make its presence felt, was about to take charge. There were also other associated problems. Although the State Government gave them one year's salary for loss of income, the Mesothelioma Organisation wanted her to sue. The Navy offered compensation and fervently hoped she would not sue. They didn't know Susie Martin.

'I was not the least bit interested, nor had any intention of suing anyone. Ever. David contracted mesothelioma doing his job. He acquired it in the course of duty,' she insisted. 'Suing was the last thing David would have wanted for his beloved Navy.' She was glad to accept the compensation offered.

Wednesday 8 August and Thursday 9 August passed in a blur. David was now in intensive care fighting for his life. Semi-conscious and to the end thinking of others, he endeavoured to mouth to Susie that she should get a cordless telephone at Randwick because then she would be able to take it anywhere. The hours passed. He was in a coma. After she had been there for three or four hours, Susie thought she would go home for a while as Vince was at the hospital with him. On her return to Randwick the telephone rang. She heard her son-in-law's voice: 'I think you should get back here quickly, Susie. It's not toe toe toe — it's knee.'

She rushed back to St Vincents realising something was terribly wrong. Penny, the nurse, told her quietly, 'He's died'.

'He can't have,' Susie insisted, 'he promised he'd wait.' She ran into his room. The first thing she noticed then was 'he wasn't puffing'. There was no sound. His struggle for breath had ended. He had asked Vince, very coherently, directly before he died, 'What should I be doing now?'. Vince had answered, 'Getting strong and well, Sir'. David's final words at 6.15 pm on Friday, 10 August 1990 were, 'Well, let's get on with it then'. A shudder. He had drawn his last breath. Brave and uncomplaining until he had not a breath left.

Sister Mary Leo, who headed the Pastoral Care Unit at St Vincents Private Hospital, said later, 'It was a beautiful experience knowing him — we shared so much together. The last time I saw him, as I walked out of the room, he saluted and said, "Night, Sis".' It had made her cry.

Everyone gathered quickly at the hospital. The family, Nick Greiner, Peter Sinclair ... Will was away skiing. Susie stayed and quietly 'talked' with David. Back home to Randwick. Vince rang the police. Five different police cars conveyed William from one place to the next and finally he arrived at Randwick at 3.30 am. It was winter. There was insufficient furniture in the house because most of it still hadn't come from storage. The family, children and adults alike, lay on pillows on the floor.

It was only when flowers and people arrived en masse and the Martin family began to console others and put them at ease that they fully realised that the nightmare was in fact a reality.

CHAPTER TWELVE

A Fond Farewell

He was the Governor who humanised Vice-Regal Office

The cathedral was packed. The State funeral and Service of Thanksgiving for the life of Rear Admiral Sir David Martin KGMG, AO, was one of the largest that Sydney has ever seen.

Believers, atheists and agnostics joined together at ancient St Andrew's Anglican Cathedral to pay their respects and to honour their late Governor. Braid and medals glistened as officers and dignitaries filed through the choristers' guard of honour.

The 1200 guests inside the cathedral included Governor-General Bill Hayden and his wife Dallas, State Governors, Cardinal Clancy and other church leaders, artist Ken Done, singer Kamahl, former Governor-General Sir Ninian Stephen, Senator Graham Richardson representing the Prime Minister, Police Commissioner John Avery, Lord Mayors, Knights and Dames, Admirals, Generals, Air Marshals, professors, judges, business and community leaders and former Governors Sir James Rowland and Sir Roden Cutler.

The hour-long service on Thursday, 16 August began at 11 am. Beforehand, a muffled peal of the cathedral bells sounded. The Right Reverend Ken Short AO, Dean of Sydney, began the scripture sentences from John and Romans. The Honourable Nick Greiner read the first lesson from Corinthians, then the choir sang Psalm 23. His Excellency Rear Admiral Peter Sinclair AO, the new Governor of New South Wales, read the second lesson from Luke. This was followed by a

Duke Street hymn after which Commander 'Polo' Owen RAN (retired) delivered the eulogy. As a survivor of *Perth*, he had been one of the last to see Bill Martin alive; now he was speaking at the funeral of Bill's son. The Sumsion Anthem sung by the choir came next. The Most Reverend Donald Robinson AO, Archbishop of Sydney, delivered the sermon, in which he said, 'We honour a man greatly loved for his strength of character, his sense of duty, his personal courage, his gentleness, his humanity. He enhanced the Office of Governor.'

The Dean led the prayers and the Reverend John Jones AM, former Principal Naval Chaplain, continued with the Naval Prayer. He had married Anna Martin and Michael Beaumont and had christened their two sons. This was followed by the blessing from the Archbishop, then the Recessional Hymn (St Gertrude) was sung by all before the procession moved to the cathedral door.

Throughout the service the Martin family remained dignified and brave. Susie Martin wore the broad-brimmed hat she had worn for the farewell drive. Was it only nine days ago? Bright red, it gave more than a hint of both David's and her own spirit. In his eulogy, Commander Owen had said, 'The achievements of this caring and courageous man could not have been attained and sustained without the unremitting love and strength of Susie'. For thirty-three years she had been there for him and with him.

Outside they stood in their numbers in a pale wintry sunshine. The mood was solemn and sad. The August wind was not quite strong enough to fully unfurl the flag that flew at half mast next to the cathedral.

The band from Scots College, David's alma mater, played 'Auld Lang Syne'; a thirteen-gun salute from the Army sounded in Hyde Park. The Royal Australian Navy Band played the Rod Stewart song 'Sailing'. It was simple and uplifting. No hype, no flowers; instead, the Sir David Martin Foundation received donations.

For the first time in the history of Australia it was gazetted that all flags across the nation would fly at half mast on the day of Sir David's funeral. Never before had this occurred for a State figure. Colin Bold, earlier that morning, gazing out a window at Government

House, observed the flags on the city skyline. They were correct, with one exception. Dialling the number of a leading Sydney hotel, he enquired of the manager, 'Haven't you forgotten something? Your flag should be half mast.' As he continued to watch, the flag was lowered.

People had begun to gather in the square outside St Andrew's Cathedral as early as 8.30 in the morning. Many of the crowd had not known Sir David Martin, but they did know what they felt for him — respect for his courage and dedication. No one spoke, they just waited. Little of the service could be heard — the loudspeakers were faulty, the last hymn was barely more than a whisper. When the coffin appeared, men took off their hats and those in uniform saluted. Draped with the flag of New South Wales, David's sword, Rear Admiral's cap and a simple posy of cream roses, the coffin was placed on the gun carriage. A 400-man guard from the Army, the Navy and the Air Force pulled the gun carriage, carrying David's casket in the procession along George Street, with silent crowds, often twenty deep, on either side of the road from Town Hall to Wynyard. William followed. Usually a non-commissioned officer carries the medals, but today David's only son fittingly filled the role instead. A proud task, a lonely task.

It was a remarkable sight. It seemed that all Sydney had turned out in farewell — hundreds of thousands of citizens of New South Wales who loved and admired Sir David. There were Girl Guides, Boy Scouts, school children, and many different Service organisations. It was a State and stately funeral, with large military involvement. Logistically, it was huge, and there were immense crowds. John Miller from the Premier's Department had organised and attended to it all — from the death notice to every last detail of protocol. Everything was ticketed and the seating pre-arranged, so many of the Martins' close friends missed out. 'They couldn't get in to the cathedral', Susie regrets. 'Many of them had to watch television in the Chapter House.'

The scene was so different from the farewell drive along Macquarie Street just the previous week. Then the thousands who lined the streets had been smiling at their beloved Governor, and he had waved and smiled back. There had been spontaneous applause. Today there was silence. Many wept.

Gradually those who were inside the cathedral drifted out and departed. Those who had waited outside for so long followed the procession or slowly dispersed. Then it was time for the private service at Northern Suburbs Crematorium. When it was over, Susie sat in the car and allowed herself a good cry.

Although he was then Aide-de-Camp to the new Governor, Colin Bold was very touched to be asked to join the Martin family service and to help carry the coffin from the hearse. He felt privileged to have escorted David to Government House on his first day as Governor and now to have carried him to to his final resting place.

Following the private service, the family went to Government House, where the Sinclairs had been in residence for only a week. On this day they were hosts to all the State Governors who were present at the service. Finally, many hours later, it was back to the Martin home in Randwick. As Susie acknowledged, 'I always knew I was going to be there on my own'.

In Hansard, on Tuesday, 14 August 1990, the Hon. E.P. Pickering, Minister for Police and Emergency Services and Vice-President of the Executive Council, said:

> The farewell that so many people gave Sir David and Lady Martin in Macquarie Street on the day of his retirement was a mark of the esteem in which they were held by the people of New South Wales. The quick wink he gave Mrs Greiner, which was caught by the television cameras as he was about to leave Government House for the last time on the final ceremonial procession up Macquarie Street, said it all about his courageous attitude towards life and duty. Even then it was perfectly plain to everyone that every move he made cost him terribly. Few outside his own family and immediate staff would ever know the enormous personal efforts he had to make to perform the duties of office during his final weeks as Governor. His impact upon the role of Governor in New South Wales will be lasting.
>
> Sir David brought to it great dignity without being in any

way distant or aloof. He brought to it a genuine warmth, friendliness and interest in all the people whom he met on the many official occasions which he attended. The Queen has never had a more able or worthy representative in this nation than the late Sir David Martin.

The Hon. J.R. Hallam, Leader of the Opposition, followed:

> It seems appropriate that Sir David, with his family history and Naval background, was appointed as Governor, an appointment enthusiastically supported by the Opposition. Had the Government not changed before the last election, a Labor Government would have appointed Sir David Martin. The announcement that Sir David had been forced to relinquish his position as Governor came as a shock to all of us. It was with great sadness we learned of the serious nature of his illness and the inevitability of what was to come. In the period following the announcement, it was patently obvious that Sir David exhibited great determination and dignity. The openness about his illness and stoicism in view of the inevitable outcome, made manifest the approachability and dignity he brought to the office of Governor.
>
> Sir David's request that the specifics of his asbestos-related cancer be made public demonstrated his concern for fellow mariners who shared his affliction. We have already seen some public benefit from that deliberate decision of the late Sir David Martin. In making explicit the link between the cancer and the asbestos used in Naval ships, he guaranteed there would be widespread public discussion about the disease, the plight of the sufferers, and the responsibility of our society toward those people. As Governor, Sir David was admired for the manner in which he attempted to open Government House to the people and to make the Governor a more accessible public figure. David Martin's unstinting application to his role as Governor and the demeanour with which he carried out his duty after the diagnosis of his illness

brought into very sharp focus the strength of his character and his commitment to his Vice-Regal duties. Sir David Martin's death as a result of an insidious disease is a tragic loss for the people of New South Wales. He will be greatly missed.

The Hon. R.B. Rowland Smith, MLC, Minister for Sport and Recreation:

If ever there was a man who deserved such admiration and praise, it was Sir David Martin. As the Governor of this State for the last 19 months he succeeded in humanising the official position with his gifts of warmth and sympathy. He had the charming ability of blending formality and humour and succeeded in divesting even the grandest occasions of their forbidding air. At the same time Sir David was very much aware of his duty as the people's representative. He brought to the position great energy and enthusiasm. While these qualities endeared him to the people of New South Wales, Sir David's professionalism and dedication earned him the well-deserved admiration of his peers. Once a Navy officer always a Navy officer — and so it was with Sir David.

Reverend the Hon. F.J. Nile, MLC, Leader of the Call to Australia Party:

I remember the first time I met him, at Government House in 1989 after he had been sworn in. As I normally do, I said to the Governor, 'You can count on our support', meaning support for him in his very responsible position as Governor. He looked me in the eye and said, 'I hope I can count on your prayers as well'. I had not expected that response from him. I felt that perhaps I should have said in the first place that he had our prayers. That was understood. I realised then that we had a unique man serving this State as Governor. He had great understanding. He understood what was happening in our State and nation. He was prepared to give whatever help he could in his position, as was the case when he held his position in the Navy. He was a leader in accepting responsibility.

The Hon. Virginia Chadwick, MLC, Minister for School Education and Youth Affairs:

He introduced a rare blend of warmth, absolute strength of character and a sense of humour. At one of his first public functions he introduced a speech by acknowledging a fairly long list of distinguished guests who were at the opening. Then with a twinkle in his eye he turned round and said, 'And anyone who is important around here'. That is probably something that has sprung to the minds of a number of us as we have gone through a long list of dignitaries at public functions. Another thing Sir David said, which certainly stands out in my mind, is:

'I do hope the people of New South Wales look to me as Governor for an example. If they do they'll get me! I think people need to look to somebody — not up to somebody — to set an example as a focus for ceremony.'

The Hon. Elisabeth Kirkby, MLC, Leader of the Australian Democrats, NSW:

In his last statement, so laboriously spoken, to the people of New South Wales, he said that he wished he had more time to achieve what he wanted for the State. I hope that he and his family know that he achieved all those aims and ideals that he talked about. The spirit of the man overcame the short period that he served as Governor. That in itself is an amazing achievement and a legacy to treasure.

The Hon. Sir Adrian Solomons, MLC, Chairman of Committees, Legislative Council:

We will all be better because our lives have been touched by both Sir David and Lady Martin. What greater tribute can be given to any man or woman?

And from the Hon. John Johnson, President of the Legislative Council:

David Martin was certainly a distinguished man among men. He had a strong sense of purpose and duty. He brought noble bearing and gentleness to his office. He graced that office in the service of this State.

What did this man have? What rare gifts or talents? The replies, taken at random, confirmed: 'He was a people person', 'He seemed like one of us', 'Every one loved him', 'He had such warmth', 'A breath of fresh air', 'A real nice bloke', 'He had no guile', 'Because of the way he handled his office and his illness', 'He was the Governor who humanised Vice-Regal office and gave it the stamp of the nineties', 'A rare and great Australian', 'A man with tremendous rapport', 'An officer and a gentleman'.

Perhaps 'He inspired others to follow' comes closest to the mark.

CHAPTER THIRTEEN

THE SIR DAVID MARTIN FOUNDATION

Hope for the future is born

On Monday 6 August 1990, his last day in office, David finalised arrangements for the establishment of The Sir David Martin Foundation — Caring for Young Australians.

As Governor of New South, Wales he had been chairman, trustee, patron and director of many organisations, ranging from the Muscular Dystrophy Association to the Royal Life Saving Society, but the Foundation was a particular dream he wished to see fulfilled. Linked with The Sydney City Mission, of which he was also patron, he recognised that this non-denominational charity with over 120 years' experience of helping the socially disadvantaged had the required expertise. He therefore saw the Foundation as an important adjunct and fundraising arm.

The Sir David Martin Foundation was officially launched by HRH, The Duchess of York, at Parliament House in Sydney in November 1990. The Foundation's main aim is to provide the funds for a rescue service and training program for young Australians who are in crisis or at risk and who need encouragement, guidance and hope. It is a grim fact that the number of teenagers caught in the destructive world of drugs, alcohol, prostitution and abuse is growing.

As Governor, Sir David had reached out to as many young people as he could, from all walks of life. Whenever he met them, he sought to encourage them to develop their undiscovered potential for the good of themselves and of Australia. He was particularly concerned about the homeless and disadvantaged who now inhabit our cities in such great numbers.

For thousands, homelessness is an everyday reality. They live day to day, without any support from their families, with little hope and no trust. Life on the streets is more painful than many of us can imagine. It's not only the fact that children are forced to huddle in doorways or look for shelter in back alleys. It's not simply their lack of food or warm clothes either. The real pain comes from the loneliness with which they live. Memories of abuse haunt them. They have no place to call home and no one to really care for them. Who can they trust?

The goals of the Foundation are to provide the financial means to enable the Sydney City Mission to:

- make contact with young people at risk, before they get caught in the destructive web of drugs and alcohol abuse, prostitution and death;
- provide accommodation, care and counselling for young people in crisis;
- provide a long-term program of character building for each young person by teaching life and work skills, leading towards self-reliance and responsibility;
- provide additional centres for homeless youth.

These troubled teenagers face rejection and loneliness. To be only fifteen years old, without any hope of escaping the vicious cycle of street life, is a tragedy. To meet the needs of these children, the Sir David Martin Foundation offers Triple Care Farm, a three-month program for those aged from fifteen to twenty-one. Situated on a lush, green 40 hectare site at Robertson on the south coast of New South Wales, it provides support and challenges for as many as twenty-four homeless young people at any one time. The many activities and education programs include carpentry, landscaping, panel beating, personal development, art, computing and living skills. They also take responsibility for the grocery shopping, and do their own cooking and cleaning.

Those at Triple Care Farm receive personal counselling from experienced youth workers and adults who are caring and consistent. This creates an atmosphere of safety and security. Because a large number of them carry the hurt and anger of abuse and family breakdown, this personal development aspect is vital in helping them learn to trust other people and, perhaps even more importantly, to trust themselves again.

Family reconciliation is another top priority at Triple Care Farm. A family therapist is on hand to help open the lines of communication between these young people and their parents, with a view to healing the damaging rifts between them.

At the end of three months, they either return home or, if that is not possible, they are placed into supported accommodation.

Over a twelve-month period, Triple Care Farm takes the first step in rebuilding some hundred broken lives, gently helping them to untangle their problems and providing them with the skills to make a positive change in their life.

The Sir David Martin Foundation also helps finance Garden Court Units, located in Wollongong, which provide supervised accommodation for ten homeless people aged from fifteen to twenty-one. The residents are involved in personal development programs, attend school or further education, and learn to become independent. In addition, the Opposition Youth Crisis Centre, located at Kings Cross, accommodates up to ten homeless young people every night. The centre also offers an important 'drop in' and referral service, and aims to move these young people as quickly as possible out of the high-risk environment of Kings Cross.

Clifton Lodge, located at Willoughby, is a group home operated by house parents. It caters for eight homeless boys and girls, aged between fourteen and eighteen. The group home provides them with stable accommodation while they complete their schooling, undertake personal development, and move towards independence.

With a total of 70 per cent of all graduates moving into work situations or going back to complete their education, Triple Care Farm is believed to be one of the most successful programs of its kind in

Australia in reaching out to young people who are emotionally hurt and troubled.

'They turned my life around', writes Kate, who, like so many other young people, fled to the bright lights of Kings Cross. She had no money and found herself trapped in a cycle of stealing and prostitution in order to survive. She also turned to alcohol and drugs to help blot out her past. Very quickly she found herself in trouble with the law. She was hauled up before a magistrate. He suggested that Kate spend three months at Triple Care Farm.

'Looking back, the three months I spent there saved my life. Apart from doing work and study, I met people who really cared about me,' says Kate. 'I made friends quickly and I even made a best friend. I liked being with the staff, too. I felt I could trust them. I was able to talk with them about the problems that I was having at home. But more than that, I felt like Triple Care Farm was a place where I belonged. It was hard to leave the farm but I learned a lot and the after-care staff still keep in touch to make sure things are okay. At the moment, I'm working as a trainee travel consultant. Triple Care Farm has really turned my life around!'

Then there is Craig, who left home when he was thirteen after a family split-up in which the children were divided between the parents. It was a very bitter, difficult time for Craig. He felt unwanted and uncared for. He ran away from home. In time, he made contact with The Sydney City Mission Youth Crisis Centre at Kings Cross, but when attempts were made to find another placement for him, he ran away again. Eventually he walked into the Crisis Centre once more. He was then twenty years old. He had spent almost the entire previous seven years on the streets of different towns and cities across Australia. Craig had never worked a day in his life. Occasionally he had gone back home, but had drifted back to the streets. He had been involved in prostitution, had a court conviction, experimented with drugs and had travelled across the country. One of his friends had died of a drug overdose three days before Craig came to the Crisis Centre for help. 'What can I do?' Craig asked. 'I know in a couple of years that will be me, but I don't know how to get out of it, I don't know any other way to live.'

Thanks to the vision of Sir David Martin, there was a program like Triple Care Farm to offer Craig. A place where he could unwind, and gain many of the skills he had missed out on. A place where he could relearn simple things, such as handling knives and forks instead of pushing food into the mouth by hand. After six months on the farm, Craig enrolled in a TAFE hospitality course and today he is in full-time employment in a hotel in Bowral and now has his own flat in the area. Such is his independence.

Wendy Barron is manager of the Sir David Martin Foundation. She is a caring one-woman band who attends to fundraising, public relations and enjoys seizing every opportunity possible to promote the Foundation's work. She works hard and loves it.

Previously a senior policy adviser, she now puts to excellent use the skills learned over the years. She sees herself as the facilitator. 'It's a very, very good Foundation and it is succeeding, and that keeps me going.' She began in August 1993 with no office, no staff and no desk. 'I just started', she says. 'Things have gone ahead quickly. It's an inspirational place.'

Susie Martin carries on the splendid work as the Foundation's ambassador-at-large with zeal. She is guest speaker at a wide variety of occasions. With gratitude, she receives cheques, and works extremely hard to continue the important legacy of Sir David, who lived his life on the virtues of service to his country, courage, fortitude and caring for the person who is down. It is a measure of the man that in those last few days, as he faced death, he gave the opportunity of life to many young Australians. David was given 'from six months to two years' to live, but was hopeful he could 'beat this thing'. He had expected to play an active role in the Foundation, not only to get it going but to keep it going. Instead, he died just a few days after setting it up. The valuable work of the Sir David Martin Foundation is an investment in the future of our children. It gives hope to young Australians now and for generations to come.

Amongst the myriad places and organisations named after David, in addition to the Sir David Martin Foundation, is a race horse (Brave

Dave), a wing of a retirement village and two sports fields. Scone Grammar School offers two memorial scholarships, Scots College a racing shell and a Pipe Banner. In Sydney in December 1990, the second Jetcat catamaran, the Sir David Martin, docked at Manly Wharf for the first time, heralding the second stage in a new era of harbour transport. The only man among many women!

There is a posthumous educational legacy from David, too. Part of his library was donated to state schools. Many of these books, personally signed, had been given to him by visiting dignitaries. Such was his interest in youth and education, he had planned to pass them on, in person, to schools he visited, but his time had run out.

In 1993, approximately two hundred of David's Naval contemporaries — many of them 'ancient mariners' — remembered him at a service of worship at the Garden Island Naval Dockyard Chapel in Sydney and the dedication of a memorial plaque. In his address to the congregation, Federal President of the Naval Association of Australia, Commodore J.L.W. (Red) Merson RAN (retired), said:

> Like many others, David Martin dedicated the greater part of his life to the service of his country in the Navy — more so, perhaps, in his case, because of his sad death from the deadly effect of asbestos at the early age of fifty-seven.
>
> His Naval service was duly recognised by promotion to high rank, with appointment to many senior postings, his award within the Order of Australia, his subsequent appointment as Governor of this state, and the honour of a knighthood bestowed on him by the Queen.
>
> His private life was equally rewarding, with a close family relationship and the love and support of his wife, Susie, his son and daughters, and their children.
>
> Of his great many attributes, he will perhaps best be remembered for those of courage and dedication, which were so very apparent in the latter days of his life and which are reflected in the memorial plaque which the Naval Association of Australia has been proud to commission in his memory.

Its inscription reads:

To the glory of God and in memory of
Rear Admiral Sir David Martin
KCMG AO RAN
1933 – 1990
Entered the RAN in 1947
Commanded HMA ships *Queenborough Torrens Supply Melbourne*
Chief of Naval Personnel 1982 – 1984
Naval Support Commander 1984 – 1988
Governor of NSW 1989 – 1990
Died 10 August 1990
A man of courage and dedication

Aft

*I love this country of ours, and the people —
this Australia and these Australians*

His Excellency, Rear Admiral Sir David James Martin KCMG, AO, left to us all a great legacy. A legacy of high ideals, of wise counsel. He delighted in making and listening to speeches and his spiritual generosity burns brightly in their texts. Through those speeches and by the example he set, he will never be forgotten. Many thought of him as a visionary, others as a prophet. Still more saw him as the man with the common touch.

Opening of Annual Conference of District 969 Rotary International

I am a great admirer of Rotary and have had a lot to do with you during my life. One of the disadvantages of life in the Navy is that we rarely settle in one place long enough to be invited to join institutions such as Rotary, which is a pity, because Navy and Rotary miss out as a result. There are not many disadvantages of life in the Navy and I must say that my forty-one years' service, and my wife's thirty-odd years (she would say very odd) as a Naval wife, have been a wonderful experience. The code we live by in the Navy bears a close resemblance to the objectives of Rotary.

'Service above self' is one of the most powerful slogans I can think of. I just wish there were a few other people, apart from those in this room, who understood the value of that message. I am aware of the symbolism of the wheel which you wear proudly on your lapel. That badge reminds me of the significance of the wheel in the development of the world — there was really no progress until the wheel was invented, and those tribes without the wheel have remained primitive. The teeth on that gear wheel give it power if they mesh and interlock with others. They transfer power and strength to other parts of human machinery. The gear wheels can be arranged in such balance and while making the best possible use of the energy available. If the gear teeth do not fit snugly with others, or if any of them are missing, then it will spin hopelessly and make no contribution to anything. I suppose I have just described to you what life is about. Life is about people and, if people behaved in the way encouraged by Rotary, then we would live in a wonderful community. But they don't behave like that and we don't live in a wonderful community.

Rotary suggests to me words like service, enterprise, ethics, worthiness, dignity, respect, understanding, goodwill, companionship, sharing, bringing together, trusting. Your central belief is serving the community and helping the individuals in it, but you are aware, as the Navy has always been aware, that, while every individual is important indeed, no individual is more important than the community of which he or she forms a part. Every community is built on the strengths of its individuals, but if they do not contribute to community or care about it, and do not interlock and co-operate with other individuals, the community will be weak, and will not hold together.

Rotary's commitment to youth is commendable. It is a thrill for me to find a body which states, clearly, the need to guide a new generation towards the ideals of service and international goodwill. I sometimes wonder if anyone in the community is trying to offer any guidance at all to the new generation. When I talk of the community, I can say to you with conviction that my wife and I have a good understanding and a deep feeling for what is going on. We get around the State as much as we can, we bring as many groups as possible to Government House, we meet those who may never achieve anything at all. We listen and learn, we try to bring people together, we spend time with those who are trying to repair and clean up our society — such as St Vincent de Paul, Salvation Army, Sydney City Mission, Red Cross, etc. We see the hopelessness and misery on people's faces and also the joy and hope of others. We try to support all the charitable groups who toil for the benefit of those who have taken the hard knocks. I could give you lots of examples of such experiences in our lives during the last fourteen months — you would then wonder, as we do, how we can also find time to meet our ceremonial responsibilities. In addition I have to carry out my constitutional tasks as the Head of State in New South Wales — I must keep in close touch with the government of the day and what they are doing, and the government must be aware that I am in close touch with what's going on in the State, and what the people want and need.

What is our overall impression after a year and a bit? A wonderful country, wonderful people, equipped with every advantage which anyone could wish for, living in a tolerant, generous, friendly land, with infinite opportunities. We see the population of this country achieving so much less than they should, and not caring enough about it. Sometimes I wonder if we are trying to give it all away or even destroy it. What caring community could possibly watch its own kids living in the streets and gutters? Its middle-aged drop-outs on the park benches, people killing each other on the roads through disgraceful carelessness, some ethnic groups (including our Aborigines) not getting a fair go; a society where a dispute like the airline crisis could be allowed to turn from an itch to a huge, festering boil? That ugly boil has spread a lot of disease; pilots' careers have been destroyed, people's work interrupted and holidays missed, companies going bankrupt, the tourist trade mutilated, Australia's reputation and self-respect damaged. Why didn't someone care enough about all these problems and why didn't someone try to solve them before they went wrong? There must have been Rotarians and other public-spirited people involved at all levels of these crises — Where were they? Why didn't they get together? Why did they let us down?

Most people were impressed at the recent beach clean-up organised by Ian Kiernan, and we saw how thousands were ready to respond when given a lead and shown what to do — that was encouraging, but it would have been better if we had never let the beach get dirty, and that can be said for all the crises already mentioned.

My wife and I are noticing that people in this country, young and old, are looking for guidance and example and they are not getting enough of it. What do the kids see as they look at the country they will inherit? Small businesses collapsing, big businesses being too smart for their own good, crime and corruption, politicians looking for votes etc, etc — what hope and faith can our children have in the future? Well, they should have lots, and let's give it to them. Rotary can give it to them.

Rotary is so highly respected, so powerful, so efficient, so happy, with such a network of communications and trust and integrity. I believe you must use those qualities and be a bit more ambitious, aggressive and brave in how you approach the rest of the community. I have said I admire the objectives of Rotary, but I wonder if they have become too bland, passive and neutral for today's society? I hope there is an unwritten aim for Rotary Australia that Rotarians should use every bit of their power to persuade, activate, motivate, guide, push, teach, criticise, and encourage other Australians to achieve all that they can, and make this the country it should be.

I have realised that my wife and I have a big job doing just that. We must be constant ambassadors for a cleaner, more honest, happy and sincere society — and that is why I am talking to you like this. I would prefer to tell you all the funny things that have happened to us in the last year or so, and share with you all our wonderful experiences, but my duty is to try and convince you that, like me, you must do more. There is no group of people in Australia or in the world better placed to spearhead the change from management to leadership, from spectator to participant, from bludger to contributor. Please do so. Please use this conference to give strength to each other and take inspiration from each other, then carry on with your 'service above self'. We need you.

Marist Sacred Heart Primary School Anzac Ceremony

Peace is precious, but it is not inevitable or automatic — it is not a right. War is awful, and Anzac Day is a time to think about what can happen if we don't manage to preserve that precious peace. But don't let anyone tell you that war is never necessary and war solves nothing. It just may be necessary at some stage to go to war in order to stop a greater evil — we had to do that in the past.

What does peace mean to you? Probably something to do with tranquillity, harmony, serenity, peace of mind. We often don't realise what peace is until we lose it, perhaps when there is a break-out of disease, fire, argument, noise, fighting.

Anzac Cove, and other battles in other places, have been places of terror, noise, injury and pain — places where peace became lost.

The young Australians exposed to such pressures knew the value of the peace they were fighting for. They had no peace, but they wanted us to have it.

In their struggle to recapture peace for us, the Anzacs became known to all the world as being cheerful, strong, healthy, unselfish, loyal, brave and always ready to help their mates. They represented the words of your school motto: 'Generosity, Faith, Courage'. Their generosity knew no limits; their faith survived the test; their courage was enough.

If we really want peace we have to stuggle for it every day. Every person, every family, every institution, organisation, group and school — our whole nation. Of course, the government has to give shape and expression to our desire for peace, our diplomats and politicians have to establish friendly relationships with other countries and our Navy, Army and Air Force have to show the world that Australia is well protected. But none of them are any use unless all Australians love their country and really want to look after it. If each of us wants it enough, the total intensity of our combined desire will be very powerful.

Remember that the integrity of our whole nation is built on the strength of each family, which in turn is built on the character of every individual person.

Peace starts in the mind of every person — you and me. Nobody can have peace of mind until he or she has done his best to sort out his own problems, built his confidence, paid his outstanding debts, done his duty, said he was sorry, and told the truth.

Anzac Day is an occasion for trying to get such peace of mind. Many of us hoped that the Bicentennial Year would have been an opportunity for us Australians — for Australia — to examine our past, try to learn from our mistakes, to make some apologies, and then to commit ourselves to doing better in future, as we do on Anzac Day, back and forward. Please remember that history is not just for us to read and learn — it is also to make. Each of you will help to make history. Please have faith in your own ability to influence that history; have courage to exert a good influence and generosity to share it.

Don't be ugly and aggressive and quick to lose your temper. Do be tolerant and do apologise when you should. But don't be weak, wet, wan, and whingeing. Remember that you have to stick up for yourself and stand up for your mates.

War takes over from peace when a bully is allowed to commit a hostile act on somebody weak and alone. If the bully were looking for somebody to take on, he would try and stay away from somebody who was known to be cheerful, strong, healthy, unselfish, loyal, brave and always ready to help their mates — Anzacs. Let's try to be like that and let's try to make Australia like that.

Pay close attention to the last line of the hymn we are about to sing: 'Let there be peace on earth and let it begin with me'.

Address to the New South Wales Council of the Ageing — Senior Citizen of the Year

Words and their meaning interest me. The misuse of words worries me. When I see the words 'ageing' and 'senior citizen', I — like many others — hear the words 'cast aside', 'given up', 'not wanted', 'over the hill', 'irrelevant', 'historic', 'prehistoric', 'flat batteries'.

And when I come here I see active people — interested, concerned, available, capable, needed — and plenty of power left in the batteries. In most civilizations, the elders of the tribe are treated with great respect and are recognised for their maturity. The elders are precious and they are a valuable resource.

'Old age' is not a helpful or constructive way to describe a personal condition. Old — so what? If a person can think, talk, listen, advise, share ideas, contribute — then, in any society, they should be considered young enough, or old enough — or just right. 'Being senior' fits well with being 'active', being 'elderly' with 'fashionable', being 'antique' with 'desirable', being 'ancient' with 'fun'.

'Retirement' is also a dangerous word. My dictionary tells me that retire means 'withdraw, to go away, to retreat, to seek seclusion or shelter'. Most of our so-called 'retired folk' should be referred to, and think of themselves, as having a change of direction in their life, a new lease of life, a new start, a fresh page, a time to consolidate and re-dedicate, to have a wonderful opportunity for a change of routine. Our country would be much stronger, more healthy, and more reliable if our elders were able to, and were encouraged to, make the contributions of which they are capable.

I am sure you realise that there is much that can be done. At one of our regular working lunches some months ago in Government House, we discussed the agonising and awful problems of those of our young people who live aimless lives away from home — lonely and desperate, often cold and hungry — involved in drugs and crime. At our lunch we had representatives of various organisations which are the front-line troops in dealing with those problems. All of them identified ways in which our older generation could help the younger generation to stay out of trouble, or get out of trouble without any risk to themselves.

Many parents are unable, or unwilling, to spend much time with their children. In many families both parents have to work and spend little time at home. Many children come from broken homes. Many parents simply don't have the courage, the faith, or the ability, to prepare children for adulthood, but there is so much that the older generations could do. Most children love and respect their grandparents and listen to them. In many Asian and European countries, the grandparents give a lot of their time to bringing up children — they have the time and the experience, and the patience and the love.

I believe everyone in Australia is seeking example and guidance and not enough have been getting it. It is my job, as the Governor, to provide as much of it as I can. Lots of other people can help, by having high standards and good values and passing them on to others. Shop keepers, taxi drivers, insurance salesmen, let alone bank managers, teachers, policemen. Most importantly, parents. And without any doubt, all those people here, the elders of our society. I am sure that nearly all of our older, senior, retired, elderly folk — what ever name we use — care about our society and I hope they can be given more opportunity to show that care and do something about it. As I said before, our elders are precious and are a valuable resource.

Opening of Annual Conference of Judges of State and Territory Supreme Courts and the Federal Court of Australia

I am very happy to be here today doing my duty as Governor of New South Wales. Thank you for showing your respect for the Office of Governor by inviting me to do that duty. For my part, I am very glad to be able to pay my respects to such an august group of people.

When I was first asked if I would undertake this task, I wondered what I could possibly say which would be of any interest or relevance.

I would like to suggest to you, and share with you, some of my hopes, opinions and ideas, naive impressions and personal observations. My thoughts may represent a layman's view, but perhaps not a typical layman, because, like most Naval officers, I have had some experience with the administration of justice. I remember the first time I was Counsel for the Defence at a trial; I was a seventeen-year-old Midshipman defending a sailor of the quarterdeck division of an aircraft carrier — he was a hairy, tattooed, huge, hung-over Able Seaman being tried summarily by a greying, lined, craggy Captain, at sea off the coast of Korea. The accused needed me desperately, and he and I knew it. I grew up that day. I remember also, as a 21-year-old Sub-Lieutenant, conducting the investigation, as the Officer of the Watch, into a case of a leading stoker, charged with being asleep at his post. I was assured by four witnesses in turn, including the ship's Senior Engineering Officer (who was twenty years my elder and better) and three Chief Petty Officers, that the man had been asleep and that was that. 'Yes, it had been pretty dark in the Engine Room, but we are pretty certain the man's eyes must have been shut' — they were out to get him. I dismissed the case, as I had to, because of lack of evidence, and I incurred the wrath of the Chief Engineer — but I was right and of course my Captain supported me.

I have been brought up in an atmosphere in which I could be involved at any time in the processes of the Naval Discipline Act: whole-hearted defence, respect for the rules of evidence, and wisdom in judgement — all essential to maintain good order and Naval discipline, to keep the ship safe and efficient, and to preserve the self-respect, safety and well-being of each person in the ship's company. In almost every one of the hundreds of cases in which I have been involved as prosecutor, defence, witness, or the officer presiding, the accused has accepted the verdict and the penalty because of respect for the trifecta: the integrity of the officer conducting the trial, the legal system, and the Naval community which maintained and protected that system.

Is this so throughout Australia today? Do people have such respect for the judge or magistrate, for the legal system and for the community? I believe they want to have such respect, but I don't think they have it.

The judge? People have been really shocked by publicity concerning some judges, said to have acted improperly. The media try to blame judges for court delays, and seek to make sensational news out of what they are pleased to represent mischievously as judges' huge salaries and their push for even more money.

The legal system? Many people worry that the legal system does not help to maintain justice. The law seems to have become so big, complicated, elaborate, that many think it inaccessible, and unable to protect the little, honest individual. On the other hand, however, there is a feeling that everyone has a right to get to court, or to appeal, at the public expense, whether or not there is a real reason to do so. Many people are encouraged by lawyers or insurance companies to sue or appeal at the drop of a hat. Other folk believe that one needs to have access to limitless funds to get a fair or prompt hearing in a serious case. We are told how the police avoid taking a case to court because of the delays, the time-consuming processes, and the impotence of the magistrate. The media would have us believe that justice is being thwarted by a frustrated, agonising, slow-moving, out-moded legal system.

If it is true that people do not have enough respect for the judge, or the legal system, how do they feel about the third leg of that trifecta — the community we live in? There are too many indications, sadly, that people don't have enough belief in themselves or confidence in our community. If this disrespect, or any of it, is real, then there is no reason why it need be deep or permanent. As with most of the ailments from which we suffer in this country, the cures are not too complicated and can be administered by ourselves, the patients. But it will take courage and strength, influence and example. That is partly your job and partly mine, and is wholly the responsibility of every one of us in Australia with a brain to think, ears to listen, and a mouth to speak with — and with faith in Australia's future.

I think your responsibility as judges is particularly onerous, and must continue to be so. I am certain I speak for the vast majority of Australians when I say that I want our judges to be looked up to and respected to a much greater degree than anyone else in the community. I want judges to be on a pedestal or pinnacle beyond reproach, free of fear and of favour, detached from many of the petty irritations and mechanical details which plague the rest of us. There is no other group of people in our Australian society who I would want to place in such a special category. I expect judges to make the hardest decisions and to bear the huge responsibility for the consequences of those decisions. (I am being careful not to say that I want judges to be 'above' or 'superior' to the rest of us because such class distinction is very un-Australian.) How can I explain that to you, and how can I indicate my sincerity in suggesting that you should be so special?

To do so I return to my experience in the Navy. Every sailor in a ship wants his Captain to bear the most responsibility, to endure the most stress and set the finest example, to have the most wisdom, knowledge and skill, to be set apart from the other officers and to be spared as much as possible from the itchy and time-consuming chores and restrictions endured by others in the ship's company. If sailors were not so self-conscious they would possibly admit that they want almost to revere, and certainly to have affection for, the 'old man'. Mind you, they do want him to be in touch with what's going on, and in tune with the needs, aspirations, the pressures and problems of every man on board. They want to know he is human and has his interests. They don't want him to be a larrikin, but they would like to think that he had knocked around a bit as a youngster — there is not much point in being 'sober as a judge' if one doesn't know what a drink tastes like.

And why do sailors want their captain to be special and remote? Because they demand of him that he be unbiased, even-handed and untainted.

I have absolutely no doubt that if the ship's community wants the Captain to be special and dignified, a bit remote, then the Australian community wants its judges to be even more so. But the reason goes far beyond the Captain's splendid isolation. The extra dimension in the judges' case is that we want the judge to be independent. I am sure I don't need to labour the point, but you may be called upon to do so. Justice is the one thread in the progress of our society that must never fray or break. Governments, political parties, wars, national disasters, even the incumbents of Vice-Regal Office, may come and go, but our society looks to its judges to be the foundation and backbone of the integrity of our nation and of our people. This cannot be sustained unless our judges are unfettered by the pressures which governments, or commercial interests, or other sections of our community, may bring to bear. The general public probably sees the judges as somewhat venerable, and I don't think this should be discouraged. Most of us yearn for the comfort and confidence which comes from knowing there is some sort of father figure standing for dependability and constancy. In times of sweeping change, we all benefit from the knowledge (or the hope) that the bench is anchored, steadfast, unswerving.

Our judges must be independent, distinctive and special, but it is not automatic or inevitable that they will be so. This independence has had to be protected in the past and must certainly be preserved in the future — at any cost. I have no doubt that our survival as a civilised community would not be possible without the independence of our judges. It is up to the community as a whole to make sure we have this safeguard. The community as a whole must see and think of the law not just as an occupation, a qualification, a profession, a public activity, a target for media exploitation or a source of income in its own right, but as the protector of justice, of the freedom of the individual, and of the future of our Australian society. The independence of judges will be questioned (and that's fair enough), but our judges must make sure the answers are provided. The independence will be challenged — then you may have to fight. You must win, even if that means stepping down briefly, with sleeves rolled up, from the pedestal on which I've just tried to place you.

So I am delighted to see you all gathered here together. I hope you have come willing and able to share your ideas, and even your doubts, fears and misgivings; to give strength to each other and to gather strength from each other; to listen and think and to gain confidence in your own wisdom and strength; to laugh and joke and to luxuriate in the release, on licence, from your normal isolation. Then please go forth and keep up the good work. Please remember that the whole country is crying out for example, for standards, ethics and ideals. You (and I) have a heavy responsibility to provide that influence.

The Governor's Prayer Breakfast

On your behalf I thank the small band of special people who suggested holding this breakfast and who have done all the work — and I mention the singers and the ushers. Their reward and recognition are in the knowledge that all of us (1 580 people) came here this morning, and that many of us will leave here more concerned, hopeful and determined, surer and braver, than when we arrived.

In my Naval career I was often frightened, and sometimes extremely frightened, but never (or not for longer than a few moments) did I feel utterly desperate or lost. I saw other Naval people around me facing serious threats, danger, doubt, risk, uncertainty and tension, that seemed crushing, but which were met with incredible physical and moral courage. With one or two very rare exceptions I never saw anybody crack, fail or run away under pressure. To see Australians acting nobly and courageously under stress is inspiring.

I think, in fact I know, that it would not be possible for Naval people to face the perils of life at sea, at peace and war, unless they had the ability and were able to give themselves wholeheartedly to their task. But they need more than that when the going gets rough.

They have faith in some thing, beyond themselves and outside their ship. Some of us have a name for that 'thing', that 'being'; I call him 'God'.

Most sailors would be too embarrassed or uneasy to put it into words. Many can't remember the last time they went to church, if, in fact, they have ever been, but they sense that they will get their extra strength and courage when they need it. And they do get it.

One of the reasons for this Prayer Breakfast is that our community is facing some serious threats (like I just mentioned: danger, doubt, risk, uncertainty and tension) which are crushing for thousands of people.

Some of the problems have become deeply established, and it worries me that we — you and I and others like us — were here when these problems developed — we let them happen ... What do I mean? Here are some examples:

- Many young Australians are living in the streets like feral animals.
- Thousands of adults — down and outs, strays — are lying around the parks like cast-offs, rejects.
- Motorists are behaving with contempt for the lives of their fellow Australians.
- Some members of our multicultural society — including our Aborigines — are not getting a fair go.
- We seem somehow to have approved, or even encouraged, temporary relationships, single parents and unmarried mothers as normal, everyday substitutes for family life.

We've let things get into a mess because — unlike the sailors I mentioned in the beginning — we did crack, fail or run away under pressure. I wonder if, now, we can find the physical and moral courage to declare our beliefs, standards and ethics, and to stand up bravely for them? Particularly in caring for others and in strengthening family life?

It is up to people like us. We can do it. The dangers can only be eliminated — extinguished — if we smother them with our own energy and commitment.

We do have the ability and we can all give wholeheartedly and generously.

What we should give are simple commodities available in abundance in Australia — respect, affection, dignity, care for our fellow Australians, and, most important example, influence, leadership.

When the going gets rough, as it is in our community today, we will need extra strength and courage. We will need to have faith in some thing, some being, beyond ourselves and outside our homes and offices. I suggest we should try asking God for the help we need and I suggest that a few prayers together — today — is a good way for us to get started.

Address to the Australia Day Council of New South Wales

In my fifty-three weeks as Governor, my wife and I have travelled a lot, have met and listened to thousands of people and developed a deep respect and affection for the population of New South Wales. We've been greeted everywhere with enthusiasm and respect — sometimes shown in strange ways. I was asked at one school if I was the Pope; my chauffeur was asked if I was Wally Lewis; I've been told I look like a German submarine captain. I've been called 'Your Majesty', 'Your Grace', 'Your Honour', and 'Mate'. One small boy said to his mother, 'Look at the poor Governor — even though he's grown up his mummy still won't let him sit in the front seat of that Rolls Royce'.

Well — that year has flashed past, and it's Australia Day tomorrow. The first enthusiasm of our New Year's resolutions may have dwindled a little, our sharp memories of the eighties might be beginning to fade, and the long-awaited nineties are suddenly here. I have some very sharp images and recent impressions in my mind. Six days ago my wife and I were exposed to the sadness, hope and courage of the people of Newcastle, and we came home feeling humble and proud. Next day we shared in the atmosphere of humour, tolerance and goodwill of some 80 000 sodden, muddy, people in the Domain during a concert called (by some comedian) Symphony under the Stars. I came home elated and, again, proud — also very wet.

But I'm getting ahead of myself. The eighties did not coast to a stop, they were marked in Australia by a series of disasters which caused great suffering and distress — the bushfires, the Newcastle earthquake, the dreadful road smashes. We were reminded that we have a feeble hold upon our lives and our possessions. But out of these awful incidents came inspiring tales of goodwill, teamwork, generosity and efficiency.

My most recent impression is of last weekend and the massive clean-up operation. It worked. It worked because there was an objective to believe in. There was a leader with the vision and the courage to take it on. There was good organisation. People joined in by the thousands because they knew the job needed to be done and each person believed that he or she could actually do something useful. So each individual did something worthwhile, and the total was indeed a grand total. Most important, the media got right behind it and gave it a fair go.

I suggest to you it is time for a few more clean-ups around here, all crying out for leadership, sense of direction, good organisation, and the feeling that each of us can actually help, and that none of us will be struggling alone.

How about a few examples? In no particular order:

- Clean-up number one: All those youngsters living away from their homes, in the back streets, the tunnels and the gutters, existing on a diet of drugs, violence, sickness and disease, cold, hopelessness and loneliness. That's a big mess to clean, but we shouldn't have let it get so fouled up. Every one of us has to try harder to bring all children up properly and prepare them to inherit Australia from us. These children are our most important assets for Australia's future, yet we are carelessly squandering those assets. It is no good blaming the teachers for not teaching them or the police for not controlling them — or the government for not saving them. In fact, I thank the teachers and the police for what they do for us.

- Another clean-up: The people we see lying under newspapers on the park benches, scavenging through the rubbish tins, clutching bottles of cheap alcohol, lacking in dignity, comfort, affection and hope. There are several organisations such as the Salvation Army, the Sydney City Mission, St Vincent de Paul, and the Wesley Mission, which are doing a wonderful job in providing some comfort to those pitiful outcasts — but wouldn't it be better if society as a whole had never let them down? A bit of affection, understanding and trust from families, neighbours, workmates (and, of course, bank managers, landlords and bosses) would have reduced the pile of human flotsam and lessened the need for salvage.

- A third clean-up: The road carnage. We all know the roads are not wide and straight enough, and that there is not enough money to fix them all at once. The driver of every vehicle knows that, too. Yet people still drive in a dangerous, irresponsible and selfish manner, killing other Australians, injuring and maiming thousands more. Every time I speak at a school (and that is often), I tell the assembled children that many of the young people I used to know are dead, and that some of the students I am addressing will be killed or wounded because some damn fool driver didn't care enough. We are all responsible for creating a better, cleaner mentality among drivers. Most of these road injuries and deaths are avoidable — it shouldn't be difficult to do some cleansing here and keep it that way — but we all have to help.

■ Clean-up number four: We still must do much more to restore, or to give, proper rights, opportunities, privileges and hope to all of our people in Australia, including, but not only, our Aborigines. There are a lot of attitudes to clean up in our multicultural Australia. The most important step is that traditional Australian custom of letting everyone have a fair go. We need a few more smiles and handshakes, and a bit more listening and sharing. Those of us who enjoy those 'nature's gifts, of beauty rich and rare' mustn't feel worried about sharing those gifts with our new arrivals who have had the courage and faith to come and join us.

We did clean up the beaches. There is no reason why we can't clean up the other ugly spots I have just mentioned — and there are many more. But wouldn't it be better if we didn't make it dirty in the first place? In my forty-one years in the Navy, I lived with that attitude because I had to. When a warship suffers because of storm, or enemy action, or if the ship is preparing for a day of special ceremonial, then every person on board turns to and gets together to make her shine and sparkle. But every sailor knows that no shop can operate successfully, efficiently, safely, and happily, unless everyone helps to keep her clean and smart all the time.

So let us take an example from Mr Ian Kiernan's Clean-Up Campaign and let's clean up Australia. At the same time, let's devote ourselves wholeheartedly to stopping it from getting messed up. If we care for our children, the derelicts, the environment, road manners, and the newest and oldest Australians, every day — then we won't need a special campaign to fix it up.

I love this country of ours, and the people — this Australia and these Australians. I hope we all do — we ought to. Let's clean it up and let's keep it that way.

SOURCES

My sources have been gathered from a wide variety of people and places. Many have been given to me by the Martin family, who kept letters and newspaper and magazine articles relating to Sir David. Every effort has been made to credit the original source and acknowledge where acknowledgement is due. I would be pleased to hear from anyone who has not been duly acknowledged. Thank you.

Chapter 1
Family papers ... 'The First Lady', source unknown ... B. Weston, 'Family Saga', *The Naval Historical Review*, June 1982 ... The Royal Australian Historical Society, 'Early Homes and Epitaphs' ... Australian Encyclopedia ... 'Honour conferred on New South Wales', *Splashes Weekly*, 24 July 1913 ... 'Rum lover led the Redcoats to topple Governor', *Sun-Herald*, 13 December 1987... John Molony, 'Not quite married — a measure of domestic bliss', source unknown ... Bankstown Historical Society, Quarterly Journal, January 1985.

Chapter 2
Interviews with Mrs Edna Little, Mrs Dempster, and Bill Hunter ... Family papers and correspondence ... Marea Stenmark, *Dad's the answer*, North Rocks Press, Sydney, 1989.

Chapter 3
Family papers and correspondence ... Interviews with Mrs Edna Little, Captain Norman Harold Stephen (Knocker) White RAN (retired), and Mr Max Jagger ... *Sydney Morning Herald* ... Tony Stephens, 'Salute to suicide mission's victims', *Sydney Morning Herald* ... Sarah Harris, 'A not-so-ancient mariner bows out', *Daily Telegraph*, 7 February 1988.

Chapter 4
Family papers and correspondence ... Interviews with Commander George Halley RAN (retired) ... Alan Zammit, 'Sons of the sea', *Naval Historical Review*.

Chapter 5
Family papers, correspondence and diaries ... Interviews with Lady Martin, Mrs Edna Little and Commander George Halley ... Sir David Martin's speeches ... Tom Frame, *Where fate calls: the HMAS Voyager tragedy*, Hodder & Stoughton Pty Ltd, 1992 ... Tony Stephens, 'Saturday Portrait — Sir David Martin', *Sydney Morning Herald*, 30 January 1988 ... Kevin Sadlier and Alan Zammit, 'From top Dad to Governor in a week', *Sun-Herald*, 21 August 1988.

Chapter 6
Interviews with Commander James (Curly) Fahey RAN (retired), Commodore Harold Adams AO, RAN (retired), and Mr Leo Duffy ... Marea Stenmark, *Dad's the answer*, North Rocks Press, Sydney, 1989.

Chapter 7
Family papers and correspondence ... Interviews with Lady Martin ... 'A surprise for Captain', unknown source ... 'Seeing their boss off in style', *Daily Mirror*, 5 December 1979 ... 'Farewell with a flourish', *Wentworth Courier*, 17 December 1979 ... Joan Marriott, 'Tresco: pride of the fleet', *Woman's Day*, 11 February 1985 ... 'Captain Martin's ancestors were all old salts', *Australian*, 1973.

Chapter 8
Family papers and correspondence ... Interviews with Commander Ken Swain AM, RAN (retired) ... The Royal Australian Navy, '75th Anniversary Celebration' video ... The Royal Australian Navy, International Naval Review Commemorative Programme.

Chapter 9
Interviews with Lady Martin ... 'Top gun sailor dragged out of the Navy', *Daily Telegraph*, 6 February 1988 ... Sarah Harris, 'A not-so-ancient mariner bows out', *Daily Telegraph*, 7 February 1988 ... Tony Stephens, 'Saturday Portrait — Sir David Martin', *Sydney Morning Herald*, 30 January 1988.

Chapter 10
Family papers and correspondence ... Interviews and correspondence with Anna Beaumont (née Martin), Sandy Di Pietro (née Martin), William Martin, and Lady Martin ... Quote from the film *Gallipoli*, screenplay by David Williamson from a story by Peter Weir ... Sir Asher Joel, *Australian Protocol and Procedures*, 2nd edition, Angus and Robertson, 1988.

Chapter 11
Family papers and correspondence ... Interviews with Mr Bill Hunter, Captain J.O. (Jo) Morrice RAN, Lieutenant Colin Bold, Mrs Sarah Renwick (née Adams), Mr Leo Duffy, and Lady Martin ... Reginald Robertson, 'The Governor of New South Wales' video ... The Rev. Dr J. Davis McCaughey AC, 'The Crown at State level', The Eighth Hugo Wolfsohn Memorial Lecture, 12 October 1993 ... Walter Bagehot, *The English Constitution*, first published 1867, Fontana Press edition, London, 1993.

Chapter 12
Interviews with Captain Morrice, Commander Vincenzo Di Pietro RAN, and Lady Martin ... Papers provided by Mrs Sarah Renwick and Lieutenant Colin Bold ... Janice Beaumont, *Sunday Telegraph*, 1990.

Chapter 13
Family papers ... Interviews with Captain Morrice, Lieutenant Colin Bold, Mrs Sarah Renwick, and Lady Martin ... Legislative Council Parliamentary Debates, Hansard, Forty-ninth Parliament, Third Session, Tuesday, 14 August 1990.

Chapter 14
Interviews with Lady Martin and Wendy Barron ... Case histories and documents supplied by the Sir David Martin Foundation ... Alan Zammit, 'Old sailors remember Sir David Martin', *Vetaffairs*, July 1993.

Chapter 15
Sir David Martin's speeches, supplied by Lieutenant Colin Bold.

INDEX

Abrahams, Esther (later Johnston), 3–13, 133
Abrahams, Rosanna, 4, 5, 12
Adams, Commodore Harold, 61, 117
Adams, Sarah, 117, 118, 120
Adelaide, 51, 112
Alfred Hospital, Melbourne, 49
All Saints Church, Willaura, 50, 74
'Annandale', 7–8, 12
Anzac Day, 116, 157–158
Ararat, 50
Armitstead, Don, 112, 132
asbestos-related disease, 125, 140
Ashmore, Admiral Sir Peter, 68, 70
Australia House, London, 54, 61
Australian High Commission, London, 54

Bantam Bay, 35
Barmedman, 122
Barron, Wendy, 148
Bates, Dr Edward, 102
Beaumont, Admiral Alan, 76
Beaumont, Elliot, 108, 131
Beaumont, Joanna (Anna) (nee Martin), 52, 57, 73, 74, 102–105, 107, 108–109, 131, 137
Beaumont, Michael, 76, 108, 137
Beaumont, Thomas, 108
Beazley, Kim, 80, 83, 91
Bellevue Hill, 54, 56, 57
Benji the dog, 109, 110, 117, 118–119, 131
Berwang, 47
bicentennial, 82, 93, 101, 158

Bligh, Governor William, 9–10, 100
Bold, Lieutenant Colin, 112, 113, 117, 119, 120, 121, 123, 127, 132, 137, 139
Brisbane, 51, 113
Burma, 45
Burma-Thailand Railway, 33
Burns, Dr Michael, 132

Cabban, Lieutenant-Commander Peter, 55
Canberra, 57, 72, 74, 95, 105, 112
Canberra Grammar School, 73
Chadwick, the Hon. Virginia, 142
Clancy, Cardinal, 136
Clifton Lodge, Willoughby, 146
coat of arms, 99
Cook, Captain James, 4, 6
Coonabarabran, 124
Coronation of Queen Elizabeth II, 46–47
Curlewis, Sir Adrian, 102
Cutler, Sir Roden, 102, 127, 136
Cyprus Emergency, 52

Daily Telegraph, 82
Dechaineux, Commodore Peter, 90
Denholm Private Hospital, 15
Di Pietro, Flavia, 107
Di Pietro, Louisa, 107
Di Pietro, Olivia, 107, 131
Di Pietro, Sandra (Sandy) (nee Martin), 52, 57, 73, 74, 102–105, 107–108, 131
Di Pietro, Vincenzo (Vince), 74, 107, 131, 134

Dodwell, Noel, 124
Done, Ken, 136
Double Bay, 16, 17, 54
Duchess of York (Fergie), 82, 144
Duke of Edinburgh (Prince Philip), 68–72, 83, 85, 87, 88
Duffy, Leo, 61–64, 125
Duffy, Michael John, 62

Edgecliff, 94, 97, 98, 111
Edgell, J.A., 31–32
Edinburgh, 31
Edyvene, Robert, 24, 100
Elizabeth Bay, 75, 94
Executive Council, 114, 129

Fahey, James (Curley Wee), 58–59, 72
Fairfax, Sir Vincent, 102
Father of the Year, 101–102, 110
Fleet Review, 80, 88
Flinders' Naval Depot, 39, 41, 44, 61, 62 *see also* Royal Australian Naval College
Fort William, 31
Foster, Commander John, 73
Foveaux, Lieutenant-Colonel Joseph, 10

Game, Sir Phillip, 127–128
Garah (Hunter family property at), 18
Garden Court Units, Wollongong, 146
Garden Island Naval Dockyard Chapel, 149
Gidginbung, 122
Gipps, Sir George, 112
Glamorgan School, 17
Glengarry, 120
Goulburn, 105
Government House, 99,

111–130, 137, 139, 140, 154, 159
Governor of New South Wales, 111–129, 130–132
Greiner, Kathryn, 132, 139
Greiner, Premier Nick, 98, 125, 131, 132, 134, 136
Griffith, 74
Guard of Honour, 132

Hallam, the Hon. J.R., 140
Halley, George, 41, 44, 45, 46, 50–51, 52, 61, 62, 116
Hallstrom, Sir Edward, 102
Hansard, obituarys in, 139–143
Harries, Admiral David (Darbo), 46
Hayden, Governor-General Bill, 136
Hayden, Dallas, 136
Hawke, Prime Minister Bob, 83–86
Hawkes, Bob, 104
Heseltine, Bill, 68, 70
Himalaya, 52
HMAS *Albatross*, 75
HMAS *Canberra*, 33
HMAS *Cerberus*, 41, 62, 64
HMAS *Cook*, 87
HMAS *Creswell*, 56, 75
HMAS *Encounter*, 29
HMAS *Kuttabul*, 75, 95
HMAS *Melbourne*, 49, 54–55, 72, 73, 83, 125
HMAS *Moresby*, 21, 31, 32, 67, 68
HMAS *Murchison*, 46
HMAS *Nirimba*, 75, 95
HMAS *Queenborough*, 57, 61, 63
HMAS *Penguin*, 75, 95
HMAS *Perth*, 21, 25, 26, 29, 31, 32–39, 42, 68, 137
HMAS *Platypus*, 75
HMAS *Rushcutter*, 27
HMAS *Stalwart*, 88
HMAS *Stuart*, 78
HMAS *Supply*, 72
HMAS *Sydney*, 46, 66

HMAS *Torrens*, 49, 67–72, 77
HMAS *Vampire*, 56
HMAS *Vengeance*, 49, 58, 59, 65, 66
HMAS *Voyager*, 54–55, 56
HMAS *Waterhen*, 95
HMAS *Watson*, 75, 95
HMAS *Yarra*, 79
HMS *Battleaxe*, 52
HMS *Britannia*, 68, 69
HMS *Devonshire*, 45
HMS *Excellent*, 52
HMS *Illustrious*, 87, 88
Hobart, 72
Hong Kong, 54, 105
Horton, Rear Admiral, 95, 132
Hudson, Vice Admiral Michael, 80, 83
Hunter, Bill, 17–21, 26–27, 113

Jagger, Maxwell (Dagsie), 37
Java, 37, 38
Java Sea, Battle of, 31, 32, 33, 35, 37
Jervis Bay, 55, 57, 75, 112, 124
Joel, Sir Asher, 81, 96–97
Johnson, the Hon. John, 143
Johnston, David, 8, 12
Johnston, George, 3–13
Johnston, George junior, 7, 8, 11–12
Johnston, Robert, 7, 8, 12–13
Joint Services Staff College, 57
Jones, Reverend John, 137

Kambala School, 57, 102
King, Governor, 100
Kirkby, the Hon. Elisabeth, 142
Knight Commander of the Order of St Michael and St George (KCMG), 98, 131
Korean War, 46, 61

Lady Penrhyn, 4, 5
Lang, Premier Jack, 127
Limb, Bobby, 102
Little, (Aunt) Edna, 15, 16, 26, 49, 74, 98
Little, (Uncle) Roy, 16, 26, 98
London, 31, 46, 54, 95, 112

McKenzie, Alan, 117, 121
McMahon, Sir William, 102
Macquarie, Governor Lachlan, 10, 11, 12, 100, 112
Malta, 52, 60, 112
Martin, (Sir) David James
　asbestos research, 125
　birth, 15
　Captain, 57, 67
　childhood, 15–21
　christening, 15
　coat of arms, 99
　Commander, 56, 58–63
　Commodore, 72
　death, 134
　Director General of Naval Manpower, 74
　Director of Naval Reserves and Cadets, 65
　education, 17, 24–26
　engagement to Susie, 50
　England, in, 45, 46–47, 49, 51–52, 54
　farewell speech, 130–132
　Father of the Year, 101–102, 110
　Fleet Operations Officer, 57
　Foundation, 144–149
　friendship with Bill Hunter, 17–19, 26–27
　funeral, 136–139
　Governor, 98, 99, 104, 111–129
　graduation, 44
　Gunnery Officer, 52, 54
　honeymoon, 51
　illness, 124–127
　Knighthood, 98, 99
　letters
　　from Kim Beazley, 91

176 SIR DAVID MARTIN

from Peter
Dechaineux, 90–91
from Sir Asher Joel,
96–97
to his children,
102–104
to his father, 23, 26–27
to his mother, 19, 42
to Peter Sinclair,
128–129
to Queen Elizabeth,
125, 126
to Sir David Stevenson,
65–67
to Susie, 68–71
Long Gunnery Course,
52, 54
memorial plaque,
149–150
Naval College cadet,
40–44
Navy promotions, 46, 52,
56, 57, 72, 74, 93
obituarys, 139–143
Order of Australia, 98,
131
RAN disaster inquiry, 55
RAN 75th Anniversary
Celebration, 80–92
Rear Admiral, 74, 75
retirement from
Governorship, 125–129
retirement from Navy,
94–100
Royal College of Defence
Studies, 73
Royal tour of South
Pacific, 67–72
school reports, 24–25
speech therapy, 24
speeches
Australia Day Council,
168–171
Governor's Prayer
Breakfast, 166–167
Marist Sacred Heart
School Anzac
Ceremony, 157–158
NSW Council of the
Ageing, 159–160
Rotary Conference,
153–156

Supreme Court Judges
Conference, 161–165
sport, 44, 105–106
story telling, 53
theatre, love of, 16
Third Australian
Destroyer Squadron,
67, 77
'Today' show, 82–83
Training Officer, 49
Washington D.C., offer
of post in, 93–94
Watch Cadet Captain, 44
wedding, 50–51
Martin, Isla Estelle (Jim),
16, 19, 23, 24, 28–32,
39, 48, 50, 57, 73–74,
133
Martin, Lady Suzanne
(Susie) (nee Millear),
48–54, 74, 94, 96–101,
110–134, 137–139, 148,
149
Martin, (Commander)
William Harold (Bill),
15, 16, 21–23, 28–39,
40, 46, 67, 137
Martin, Lieutenant
Commander William
(Will), 54, 57, 74, 76,
103–106, 131, 134
Matapan, Battle of, 32
Melbourne, 40, 50
Melbourne Grammar
School, 61
'Mena' (Hunter family
property), 18–19
Menzies, Prime Minister
Robert, 44
Merson, Commodore
J.L.W. (Red), 149
Mesothelioma
Organisation, 133
Millear, Spencer, 49, 51, 54
Millear, Sylvia, 48, 50, 51,
53, 112, 132, 133
Miller, John, 138
Mitchell, Terry, 67–68
Morrice, Captain Jo, 117,
118, 124, 131
Mountbatten, Earl
Richard, 68, 69, 71

Murray, Mrs (Jim's
mother), 17, 29–30
Muscular Dystrophy
Association, 144

Naples, 48
Narooma, 119
Navy *see* Royal Australian
Navy
New South Wales Corps,
8–11
Newcastle earthquake, 124,
168
Newcombe family, 27
Nichols, Charles, 12
Nile, the Hon. F.J., 141
Norfolk Island, 7
Northern Suburbs
Crematorium, 139
Norway, 45
Nowra, 104
Nyngan floods, 127

O'Callaghan, Gary, 102
Oliphant, Sir Mark, 67
Orcades, 47, 94
Order of Australia, 98, 131
Owen, Commander Polo,
36, 137
Palembang, 38
Paterson, Captain William,
8, 10
Phillip, Governor Arthur,
4, 6, 7, 8, 100, 112
Phillip Island, 41
Phillips, Captain Mark, 69,
70
Pickering, the Hon. E.P.,
139
Pollard, Professor Alfred,
102
Port Said, 49
Portsmouth, 47, 52, 54
POW camps, 37, 38, 39
Prince Andrew, 82
Princess Anne, 68–72

Queen Elizabeth II, 46–47,
68–72, 79, 98, 107
coronation, 46–47
David's impressions,
68–72, 79

INDEX *177*

David's letter to, 125, 126
letter to HMAS *Torrens*, 71
tour of South Pacific, 68–72

Rakuyo Maru, 33
Randwick, 133, 134, 139
Red Cross, 155
Richardson, Senator Graham, 136
Robertson, Captain R.J., 55
Robertson, Reg, 113
Robinson, Reverend Donald, 137
Rome, 52
Rose Bay, shelling of, 18–19
Ross, John, 36
Rowland, Lady, 127
Rowland, Sir James, 111, 122, 127, 128, 136
Royal Australian Naval College, 29, 33, 40–45, 56, 118
  David as cadet, 40–44
  entrance exam, 26, 40–41
  Selection Committee, 40
Royal Australian Navy, 80–92, 100, 106, 133–134, 153
  administration of justice, 161–164
  Band, 137
  Fleet Review, 80, 88
  Naval Board, 34
  Naval Discipline Act, 161
  Navy Office, Canberra, 65, 72, 74
  Naval Supplies Centre, Zetland, 95
  1964 disaster, 54–55
  75th Anniversary Celebration, 80–92
  World War II battles, 31–39
Royal College of Defence Studies, London, 73
Royal Life Saving Society, 144
Royal Naval College, Greenwich, 46, 56, 61

Rum Corps, 8–11

Sangiang Island, 36, 37
Scone Grammar School, 149
Scots College, 17, 18, 24, 26, 43, 99, 110, 113, 120–121, 137, 149
  David's reports, 24–25
  Glengarry, 120
  Jim as Assistant Bursar, 24
  Robert Edyvene, principal, 24, 110
Scouts, 42, 124, 132
Short, Reverend Ken, 136
Simpson, Mr, 43
Sinclair, Rear Admiral Peter, 127, 134, 136, 139
  David's guide for, 128–129
Singapore, 38
Sir David Martin Foundation, 144–149
Smith, the Hon. R.B., 141
Solomon Islands, 79
Solomons, Sir Adrian, 142
Spain, 45, 74
St Andrews Cathedral, 136, 138
St Stephens Church, Sydney, 31
St Vincent de Paul, 155, 169
St Vincents Private Hospital, 132, 133, 134
Stephen, Sir Ninian, 81, 87, 98, 136
Stephens, Captain Duncan, 55
Stephens, Tony, 55
Stevenson, Vice Admiral Sir David, 65
Strathhaird, 45
Strathmore, 46
Stretton, Major General Alan, 102
Sunda Strait, Battle of, 26, 31, 32–39
Sutherland, Doug (Lord Mayor), 81

Swain, Commander Ken, 77–86
  RAN 75th Anniversary Celebration, 80–92
Sydney City Mission, 144, 145, 155, 169
Sydney Harbour Bridge, 87, 88
Sydney Morning Herald
  1964 Navy disaster report, 55
  Roll of Honour, 31
Sydney Opera House, 81, 87, 128

Telok Betong, 38
Thode, Lieutenant John, 35, 37
Tjilatjap, 37
'Today' show, 82–83
Toorak Ladies College, 44
Topper's Island, 37
'Tresco', 75–76, 97
Triple Care Farm, 145–148

USS *Chicago*, 34
USS *Houston*, 34, 35, 36, 37
USS *Missouri*, 87, 88

Varley, Mike, 46
Vaucluse, 57
Vaucluse Public School, 57

Wagga Wagga, 124
Waller, Captain Hector (Hec), 22, 33, 34, 35, 36, 37, 42
Waller, John, 42
Warren, 49
Watsons Bay, 17
Wellington, 72
Wentworth, W.C., 12
West Indies, 45
Westernport Bay, 41
White, Captain Norman (Knocker), 33–37
Widerberg, Bill, 82
Willaura, 49
  All Saints Church, 50, 74
Williams, Noel, 18
World War II, 41, 42, 68, 87
  naval battles, 32–39
Wran, Neville, 81